Profit Now for Your Restaurant

Turn Your Lagging Business Into a Successful and
Lucrative Money Making Machine

Profit Now for Your Restaurant

Turn Your Lagging Business Into a Successful and Lucrative Money Making Machine

Darren Takenaga

Dedicated to all the business owners who open the doors in the morning, close at night, and stay up another eight hours preparing for the next day.

Table of Contents

Table of Contents

Table of Contents

Preface

This book was written for owners, stakeholders, and decision-makers of small restaurants, most affectionately called "mom and pops." I myself am a restaurant owner and understand the very limited time in the day and night to focus on any one aspect of operations and restaurant success.

A suggestion on approaching the content in this book is to skip around. Thumb through the pages and pick a chapter to implement. However, it will be a more effective journey if you read the introduction. Then, if you have the opportunity, read the book cover to cover. There are various details sprinkled throughout the book that will give the depth and understanding that was intended.

It is very easy to read parts of the book, and then nothing happens. Minimally, please try out some of the chapters. These chapters were written from real-world experience. They work for me. I am confident they will work for you.

Enjoy the journey.

Acknowledgments

This book reflects my life and could not have happened without others that affected my life path. My parents—Mom—Phoebe, who I miss every day. She taught me that being a teacher is one of the most satisfying endeavors. Her love of travel rubbed off on me. My Dad—Eugene—who continues to inspire me for the challenges he faced in life and the successes that were born out of perseverance, tenacity, forgiveness, and humor.

Thank you to my favorite brother and sister and then to my other brother and sister. My best friend and wife, Sunutta whose support and guidance have brought me on an incredible journey that brings smiles to the past, exhilaration for the present, and anticipation to the future. Natalie, my daughter, whose example of how life can be enjoyed and lived. Always with a smile and laughter in her talk. One can never be sad around her.

Mike Robak never ceases to amaze me with his kindness, integrity, honesty, and just how creative and smart any one person can be. There are master marketers in this world who do not know me, but I thank them for documenting and teaching their craft. A small list includes Gary Halbert, Joseph Sugarman, Jay Abraham, Claude Hopkins, Chet Holmes, Joe Polish, Dan Kennedy.

Introduction

The Mindset and the Reality

Statistically, for the general public, when dreaming of owning their business, a restaurant is at the top of the list. And this makes sense because of all the media attention this type of business receives. For example, one does not need to look far to see cooking shows related to competition, food prep, restaurant operations, and the list goes on. Somehow, these shows convey the glamour and fame of owning a restaurant.

I came from a background in marketing. At first, it was a hobby because I was intrigued by the power marketing and advertising have over humans when it comes to decisions, movement of goods, and emotional directives. Then marketing became a more serious endeavor when I applied my learnings to real products. In the past, I helped to market plush toys, dolls, novelties, and souvenirs. Along my life path, I picked up a restaurant, and eventually, within two years, had three restaurants in my portfolio.

I myself got caught up in this current thinking of restaurant ownership. Whenever people I meet find out that I own restaurants, there is a glimmer in their eye. Questions abound about what it is like to own a restaurant. Have I met famous people that have dined in my restaurants? What is it like to be an owner of restaurants? The questions continued.

At first, I carried over my skills of marketing into my restaurants. Business grew, and I was comfortable with the profits that came with ownership. But then, I stopped marketing the businesses. Reflecting, I think that it was more of a time-management issue. I just didn't have the time to focus on the marketing. I started working on upgrading the interior, creating new menu items, and working on new exciting ways to amaze my clients. Besides, the restaurants were growing in sales. Or maybe I wanted to take home more money. This could be accomplished by cutting costs. And marketing is a cost? Right?

Once I started the marketing and advertising, something strange happened. The restaurants still grew in sales for another four months. I became even more complacent. I felt I was king of the restaurant empire. And then that is where things became noticeable. Sales dropped literally overnight; I started to reflect on what was happening. The economy was still booming. The menu didn't change. The prices didn't change.

Then I read, among my marketing resources (see end of book), that if marketing is stopped, then a business can expect to lose 10 percent of its client base per month, called attrition. This attrition can sometimes be the fault of the business. But other times, it is not. People move away, change preferences, have other life events that essentially stop them from doing business.

Introduction

That once-thought-about attrition hit me upside the head. I suddenly realized that my stopping the marketing affected my businesses in a drastic way. Once that realization occurred, I started marketing and advertising, and once again, my businesses started to gain traction and were on a corrected path to profits and fun. You see, when a business is not doing well, the fun and glamour is gone. It becomes a dreaded thought literally twenty-four hours a day. It consumes you of all energy and any creativity or capability to derive a solution to correct.

Most owners, at the point of losses, start blaming everybody but themselves. The clients, team members, food costs, service, overhead, and the taxes all become subject as answers to business losses. But once an owner looks in the mirror and blames that image, suddenly power comes back and a solution arises.

The big takeaway is that you and I, as restaurant owners, need to focus on marketing. Marketing is paramount. I would even go out on a limb to say that marketing is even more important than food and service aspects of the business. Before, it was possible to have a good location, great food, and great service for a restaurant to succeed. But times have changed. Yes, marketing is not the end-all-be-all of a restaurant business. But please know and remember that marketing is an essential focus to help ensure the success of this business.

The Power of Three

Do you remember the episode of *School House Rock* where the number three was highlighted? It was called "Three is the Magic Number." Three is a powerful number. You need at least three legs to support a chair or a table. Yes, three is a magical and powerful number. With restaurants, three works in the same way. You just need to remember three powerful statements that lead to three focuses. If you improve on any of the three focuses, there is a powerful effect on helping with the success of your business.

The first focus is to always increase the number of clients that you have. Remember that there is a constant attrition pulling at your client base. There are different reasons for losing clients, but accepting the fact that you are losing clients kind of lights a fire under you to be mindful that the bucket is losing water. And you must be constantly filling this bucket with water. Another way of looking at this is that increasing clients also increases client spending. At the quantitative level, if only 1,000 clients walk into your restaurant a month and spend $10, then that equals $10,000 in gross sales. Per the first focus, increasing client visits an additional one hundred clients, then that equates to an additional $1,000 if the average ticket is $10. Throughout the rest of the book, when first focus is mentioned, that entails increasing your customer base.

The second focus is to increase the sales per client visit. It makes sense. If your average ticket sale is $20, you are going to gross a certain amount a month. For example, for the sake of easy math, 1,000 clients per month walk into your restaurant. Gross sales are $20 multiplied by 1,000 clients. That is gross sales of $20,000. Per the second focus, if you increase sales by $1, then the 1,000 clients equate to an additional $1,000 in gross sales. However, if you take the same number of clients that visit your restaurant and increase spending by another dollar, per ticket spent is $22, which equates to another $1,000. Throughout the rest of the book, when focus number two is mentioned, then this entails increasing the sales per ticket or transaction.

The third focus is to increase the number of times your current clients come back to do business with you. Throughout a given year, especially for restaurants, if your service and food is on par and meets the needs of your clients, they repeatedly come back. The goal of this third and important focus is to increase the times the client does business with you. Quantitatively, if the client comes into your restaurant two times a month and spends $20, this equates to $40 a month or $480 in a year. Are you able to see, just thinking in this mindset, how numbers can be forecasted and offer increased motivation toward increasing your business success?

Anyways, what if the client comes back with an additional visit per month? That entails to an additional $20 a month and $240 in gross sales per year. This grand total is $720 compared to the previous example of $480 in gross sales. And this is just for one customer. Then you can carry out these numbers to your total customer base and really see that the power of increasing these numbers by a small percentage affects your bottom line. Throughout the rest of the book, when there is mention of focus three, we are increasing the number of visits by existing clients.

Section One – The Three Focuses

In this first section, we're going to take a look at the three aforementioned focuses in a little more detail. You'll learn tips for increasing your client base, increasing the amount your clients spend (increasing the sales per transaction), and increasing the amount of repeat customers you have. I've either personally used or seen these strategies used in order to boost a business's marketing prowess, and I can attest that they do work.

Focus One – Increasing Clients

If you're unable to increase the amount of clients coming to your establishment, then you won't be able to convert them into repeat clients who spend more with each visit, so it only makes sense to begin by figuring out how to draw more hungry customers into your restaurant. So in this section, you'll learn some nifty marketing ideas that will pull clients in.

Bandit Signs

This strategy was mentioned a little in another chapter. But here, it is detailed in more depth. Bandit signs are the little plastic signs with metal stakes that often are metal rods. Most prominently found during election time, bandit signs are mini billboards. People read them.

If you see these signs in your area, chances are that there is a printer who specializes in this type of printing. Worst case scenario is that you can find resources on the internet ,but shipping tends to hamper the item cost.

There are some takeaways, as with a lot of these marketing weapons in this book. Remember that most marketing campaigns need to have an offer. If there is not an offer, people don't care.

Focus One – Increasing Clients

I've seen a lot of bandit signs in which there is the name of the business. Sometimes, there is the service offered such as "pool cleaning" or "lawn service." This is good if someone needs the service at that moment. It's a numbers game for sure. Chances are that someone will need that service. But why not increase the chance someone responds to your sign?

Besides offering the service, offer a reason to act. For example, offering a free recorded message as to why it might be dangerous to go swimming or five ways to decrease the cost of owning a lawn. Free recorded message. Or receive a free report by going to a website.

Do you see that even if you already have a pool service or lawn service, there is an increased chance of getting more inquiries? If I had a lawn service, I would at least be open to what the message has to say.

In the restaurant business, you can offer a free gift card by calling a free twenty-four-hour recorded message or going to a website. Another message that has worked for me is offering a free drink or appetizer by listing the restaurant name.

The caveat is that you need to research your city ordinances. In my city, it is all right to place bandit signs. However, it can only be done on the weekend. Then it must be collected before the weekend ends or risk a fine. A little bit of a headache for sure. But it is worth the effort.

Chamber of Commerce

Every city has a local Chamber of Commerce. It is almost required that every small business should be a member because of the benefits. First, you will be among like-minded individuals that can help each other in growing your businesses. When you collaborate with businesses in a different category, you can partner with helping each other out with referrals and marketing.

Each Chamber of Commerce is different, but mine offers ribbon cuttings and listings in printed publications and the website. With the ribbon cuttings, the business doesn't have to be just opening. My chamber will even do a ribbon cutting if you upgrade your dining room or make a change that can justify "newness."

With the website, SEO aspects are beneficial. They can link your website to theirs, which gives props to your restaurant as an authority site. The search engines consider the Chamber's site as an important site, which gives it higher ranking. By having your site linked to the Chamber's, you get higher rankings because of the association with the Chamber. The Chamber is indirectly referring you through the search engines as a restaurant that should be patronized.

The Chamber also has a central office for meeting and administration. You can place your fliers in the office with promotions for individuals that are members of the Chamber. I also have made arrangements to have meetings in my restaurant. The Chamber of Commerce is there to help and is usually receptive to any suggestions that benefit both parties.

There is an affiliation benefit. Chamber members tend to do business with each other. I myself had my car repaired and have eaten at establishments that were Chamber affiliated. And in return, I have had Chamber members and even the mayor dine in my restaurant (the mayor was an officer of the Chamber).

By being a Chamber member, a plaque is given to the member (I prominently display on the wall and use the logo wherever I can). The logo is placed on any printed, internet, and marketing materials to give credibility and community involvement support.

As a side note, if you can become a member of any other organizations such as Kiwanis, Rotary, a local charity, or the Better Business Bureau, you can often use the logos in all your materials. Credibility, even at the subconscious level, helps with the overall perception of your restaurant.

You can work on the authority aspect. You can have a presentation at one or more of the meetings on marketing a small business. You can write articles or submit one of your original content to the Chamber's printed publication. If writing an article, remember to send readers to your website or offer a special to Chamber members.

Delivery Partners

Offering delivery is almost becoming mandatory. People are always looking for convenience in their lives. Having food delivered to their home offers that convenience when it comes time to satisfy their hunger.

Before, a restaurant would have to negotiate many variables to even make delivery a possibility. Variables such as liability insurance, having reliable drivers, and figuring out the logistics was sometimes too much of a headache to offer delivery.

Now, restaurants are being offered these services through third-party companies. Gone are the days of figuring everything out. Now, an order comes into your restaurant usually via a tablet. The restaurant fulfills the order. Then a driver comes to pick up the food and delivers to the customer.

Seems too easy. It is, but there is a downside. The other side of the coin is that there is a commission that is deducted from the sale. With some companies, the commission can be as high as 30 percent. That can take a bite out of the bottom line.

The argument is that a sale is still better than not getting the sale. A slim profit margin is still better than no sale. Also, if your competitors are offering delivery, the client could possibly order delivery through them versus your restaurant. Therefore, your dining room and walk-ins can still be lower.

However, there is a way to justify cost on the marketing argument. These companies are not unique with this business model. In fact, there are six delivery companies competing for the same company.

Therefore, if the delivery companies are competing, then they are doing everything they can to gain market share. They are spending their marketing dollars toward gaining restaurants and helping the restaurants get customers.

For example, you will find that these companies' marketing spending is found on all the search engine advertising, social media, and review sites. They rank well with SEO, and therefore, any restaurant under their program benefits as well.

Focus One – Increasing Clients

Stay in contact with your assigned representative of the delivery partner. He or she is looking out for your success. You can ask for printed promotions that can be offered to your clients. These promotions are usually in the form of first-time order discounts or free delivery.

That translates to your restaurant getting new clients through the marketing of the delivery partner. If you consider the commission as customer acquisition, you can calculate the cost per customer. It is important that you are able to reach out to the customer and acquire their contact information and get them into your database.

There are several ways to entice the customer to subscribe or sign up. Discussed in another chapter, package inserts are one way to contact the client. It can be as simple as a printed flyer explaining the different programs you offer. And it can get more complicated with other subscribers joining you with offering promotions, sales, and offerings.

Another way to get customers to notice your programs is to create labels that adhere to your packaging. The client cannot help but read the label and then act on it. Remember that the label needs to have a headline, benefits, call to action, and deadline. Think of the label as a small direct mail piece (detailed chapter is found in this book).

There is a downside that needs to be mentioned. Since your restaurant will be advertised and placed in a directory, a customer that goes there to order will find all your competitors as well. This is bad news for you because you will be competing with everyone in your category and everyone not in your category.

And in this situation, unless you offer food that is unique, the determining factor will probably be price. Therefore, it is important that you reach the customer first or be first in mind.

One way to overcome the competition choices is to have your own website with the delivery link. Another option that is recommended is to create a website that focuses on delivery. It should have the feel and look of a company offering information on delivery options in your area. But the only option will be your restaurant. Please refer to this topic in more detail in another chapter of this book.

Another way to be the first choice with the delivery option is to create a magnet or other advertising specialties. The magnet, in my testing, works well because a number of clients work in an office setting. There is usually some sort of wall surface or filing cabinet made of metal. A colorful magnet serves as a mini billboard reminding the person of your delivery option.

Direct Mailing

Seems counterintuitive to use direct mail, snail mail, and physical mail currently. But to ease your thinking, the internet and emails are used in other marketing campaigns in this book. Direct mail is still a powerful medium in which to find clients for your restaurant. If you want a little comfort that you will not be using an outdated tool, check your mail regularly. There was probably a mailing from Google. Why would Google send a mail piece when they control the interspace? Case closed.

The post office, in recent years, has become more sophisticated and more attractive to small business owners with direct mail offerings. Now you can dial in your mailings with more of a rifle approach rather the shotgun approach. You can make your mailings more cost-effective by picking mailing zones.

You can start off with the zones that demographically make sense for your business. For example, maybe a mailing zone has more affluent residential housing. Or a zone has more businesses. You can test zones and track the effectiveness of the zone. If one zone is more effective than the other zones, you can concentrate more of your marketing efforts toward that zone. Over time, you will start to get a better description of your ideal client through age, occupations, desires, wants, fears, etc. Only through understanding your ideal client base will your marketing message become more effective.

Another way to use direct mail is to contact a list broker. A list broker's main purpose is to compile mailing lists of variables of your choosing. For example, you can request a mailing list of all males who like to play basketball. Or you can request a mailing list of all pet owners that live within a five-mile radius of your restaurant. Are you getting excited?

The list I like to use is two household income and homeowners in their mid-thirties to late forties. Another list I like is homeowners, two household income, and just moved into the neighborhood within six months. You see, new movers are looking for new habits. These habits include where to eat. They are looking and receptive to trying new things and establishing their favorites.

The mailings are limited by your creativity. However, I suggest you stop here and turn to the chapter titled Copywriting 101. There, you will find a simple hack to create a decent mailing piece. The mailing piece I found effective is to offer a free entrée. The entrée coupon is printed within the mailing piece. It is required that the client brings the letter with the coupon attached. Each coupon is coded to a certain mailing zone.

When the client comes to the restaurant, they are asked to complete an information form asking for name, address, birthday, and email address. This is a good tradeoff for giving a free entrée for their contact information.

It takes three to five visits before a client adopts your restaurant as a habit. Therefore, it is very important that the client comes back. The sooner the better. Sometimes, on the first visit, after completing the contact form, a buy-one-get-one (BOGO) coupon is given. Even more powerful is in a couple of days the new client receives a thank you letter in the mail with the BOGO coupon attached.

But also, the relationship has started. Henceforth, the client receives a newsletter, birthday promotion, mailings, and other correspondence to keep the client active in your offerings.

Door Hangers

Door hangers, as the name implies, are printed matter that are hung on a door. There are upsides and downsides with this strategy. For restaurants, this is a way to pick neighborhoods and demographic areas nearby. Door hangers do get read.

Again, the big takeaway is that you need to be able to track this campaign. The easiest way is for the client to bring the door hanger with them to the restaurant to redeem. Then register their contact information to finalize the redemption. Remember to have a promotion, call to action, and most importantly, a deadline.

Although testing will prove or disprove, the promotion needs to really be pushing your cringe level. For most owners, the default promotion is 10 percent or 20 percent off a purchase. However, this is so common that clients are not affected by this discount anymore. Offering a free entrée or minimally buy-one-get-one-free (BOGO) is getting better. My suggestion is push your cringe level and test a promotion that you would consider extreme or over the top. In the end, a dollar invested must return the dollar.

The downside is taking the time to implement this strategy. It is often a challenge for the owner to door hang themselves. However, you can pay people to door hang. This is all and well if you check on their work. I have known door hangers to do a couple of houses and slow down. They have also thrown away door hangers and say the job was done. Hopefully, this won't happen to you. I'm just giving you the heads up.

Fish Bowl

This is not new, and you have probably seen this in other restaurants you dine at. But it still works. Called fishbowl marketing, you purchase a goldfish bowl. You then create a small sign taped to the fishbowl that states "Drop Your Business Card for a Chance to Win Four Free Lunches and Drinks."

I like to give away lunches because that is when I have most businesses come in for lunch. They usually have business cards and readily drop it into the bowl. I like to offer four lunches because, often, they bring colleagues and word-of-mouth referrals increase.

Focus One – Increasing Clients

There are some important points that will help with this promotion. First, always keep some business cards in the bowl. This is important immediately after a card is drawn. An empty fish bowl looks scary to the first card dropper. Nothing attracts a crowd like a crowd.

Second, I have a chalkboard and like to post the winners every month. It gives the impression that I'm really giving away lunches and not just keeping the cards. The side benefit is that the winners like to see their names posted and openly brag about it (at least for a month).

Third, these names should be kept in a separate client list. This is even more important if you offer catering. Around the holidays, or any time of the year, I like to send a special mailing to this list with catering offers. Businesses do eat in, and if they know you offer catering, you will be at least in front of the short list. The side benefit is if the colleagues have won one of your lunch promotions, they are great advocates for your restaurant among their colleagues at their business.

Fourth is awesome. Even though there is one winner of four lunches a month, I still make the rest of the participants winners. I reach out to them and explain that I'm sorry they didn't win first place. But there is an unannounced second place. Second place winners receive some sort of consolation. The second-place winner has no idea that everyone won second place. It still feels exclusive. I tend to mix it up with a free soft drink, discount, and anything that helps to bring the clients back into the restaurant.

Of course, you need to track everything. Everybody is asked to bring the printed letter, coupon code, gift card, or anything else to track and analyze the data. A dollar invested must return a dollar or more for every marketing effort.

Referral Programs

It is a struggle to get new clients in the door. But one of the most powerful ways to get new clients is through referrals. For someone who hasn't tried your restaurant, hearing a recommendation from an acquaintance is a powerful way to get them in the door.

Referral programs can be a challenge. However, one of the easiest ways to get referrals is by monitoring conversations. If a client remarks positively about your food and service, the next sentence is to say thank you and then ask the client if they know someone who would enjoy the experience as much as they did. Often, you will get a reply of yes. The challenge, though, is if they actually will refer your restaurant.

But it's a numbers game. If stated often enough, you will get referrals and clients coming to the restaurant through the recommendations.

A structure that can be put in place is when the positive conversation happens, the team member gives a card to the client. The card looks like a gift certificate with a note stating that this gift is given from (name and address) to recipient with a value of $10 to be used at your restaurant.

Face value can be tested, but $10 is a high enough amount to garner someone to act. Also, you need to mention that there should be a call to action and deadline. The recipient needs to include a name and address to redeem.

When the new client brings in the gift certificate, this signals to the team members that this is probably a first-timer. When confirmed, a welcome package is given with a reward, birthday, and newsletter sign-up sheet. There is also a bounce-back coupon to ensure that the new client comes back.

To ensure the experience is continued, a thank you card is sent to the new client. And most importantly, the giver of the gift certificate is sent a thank you card for the referral. It is optional to include a coupon. But in past tests, the giver is completely happy to have been recognized for the favor. With the coupon, the experience can seem like it was purchased or cheapened.

I think if you approach client relationship with gratitude, you will find that your marketing campaigns become more powerful and effective. Remember to practice the gratitude attitude.

Another variation is to have an official referral program in which a card is given to the original referring client. The client completes the card and gives it to the acquaintance. Then, when the acquaintance redeems, the card is collected and placed in a raffle box. The referring client then has a chance to win an awesome prize. This definitely increases participation and referrals.

Free Lunch

This program is titled "No Such Thing as a Free Lunch." This marketing program is designed to get professionals in the door. These professionals include doctors, lawyers, teachers, etc. The perception is that these professionals have their own network of contacts and clients in which to refer.

Focus One – Increasing Clients

There are several ways to bring the professionals into your doors. The direct mail approach is to craft an invitation letter offering a free lunch. These keywords can make a great headline because of the term "No Such Thing as a Free Lunch." But with the headline, you can use the approach of "There is such thing as a free lunch." Remember, with direct mail, you want to continuously test effectiveness of your marketing campaigns.

The biggest tip is that you don't want to offer a discount or something frivolous such as buy-one-get-one-free appetizer or drink with purchase. You want to make a big impact and make an offer they cannot resist.

Many people balk at the idea of giving away free food. But if you analyze the numbers, you will see that the average client comes back repeatedly to your restaurant. This entails a value much more than a single visit. The lifetime value of a client can be in the hundreds and thousands of dollars.

Another requirement is that you track and analyze the effectiveness. A dollar spent must be returned as breakeven or profit. A great way to track is to make sure that the client brings the coupon with them. Also, you want to make sure that you enroll the new client into your various programs such as rewards, birthday, and newsletter subscriptions.

Through time, you want to keep these contact names of professionals in mind when developing your referral system campaigns. Again, these professional have their own network, and if you can enchant these clients, the referrals will grow.

Focus One – Increasing Clients

Note that even though professionals are the target for this marketing campaign, there are many more segments in which to focus your marketing efforts. There are law enforcement, firefighters, real estate agents, and the list goes on.

Another marketing program is to map out the various companies in your immediate zone. Look for companies with a sizable labor force. With a larger workforce, there will be the administrative support. This administrative support is those that are able to go out to lunch and, hopefully, to your establishment.

To start the process, you can implement reciprocity. With reciprocity, you give away something free. The client then feels obligated to reciprocate by purchasing from your business. That is why, in the malls and big box stores, you will find employees giving away free samples. If you ever observe shoppers getting free samples, you will see that a large number will then reach for the product to purchase. It's human nature to balance the scales.

With this program, you want to pack lunches in brown sacks (similar to school lunches) or to-go boxes. It doesn't have to be the full portion but enough to be satisfied with the eating experience. Along with the lunches, you will want to add your business card, flyer, magnet, and any other redemption offer so that you can keep track.

The side benefit is that your company will be part of the conversation for catering opportunities. You want to make sure that your information included with the lunches also mentions strongly your catering capabilities and offerings.

Free Wi-Fi

Offering free Wi-Fi can still be a powerful component in gathering contact information from your guests. As the name suggests, a client that walks into your restaurant has access to free Wi-Fi. Currently where it seems everyone is subscribed to the internet, there are those that still need to be aware of data subscription caps. Turning off their internet access in favor of your Wi-Fi is still an option.

Setting up free Wi-Fi can be approached several ways. One way is to give your password away for your internet access. However, this can be scary. People can grab internet operations that you yourself are doing, such as online banking or other information-sensitive work. The other downside is that there is really no way to capture guest information. If you are offering it as a convenience, then maybe this is the way.

However, we marketers are in the business to track and test. There are third-party services that provide the hardware and the platform to offer free Wi-Fi. With the process, the guest provides an email to log in. That email can then be used to conduct marketing promotions such as sending coupons, correspondence, and any other marketing weapon discussed in this book.

Another powerful aspect with using third-party Wi-Fi is that their platform keeps track of the number of visits, number of new subscribers per time period, and other data that can really help with your marketing campaigns with Wi-Fi or otherwise.

The caveat to this marketing weapon is that it can really be effective or not be effective, or something in between. For me, I was able to test free Wi-Fi with my different restaurant locations.

One of the restaurants had a handful of new subscribers per month. Another restaurant experienced the opposite. There were hundreds of subscribers per month. I canceled the one restaurant because the acquisition cost per guest didn't make sense compared to the subscriber fee. That's why testing and metrics is important.

But all was not lost. I was able to get a better insight on my clients. It appeared that the restaurant that experienced poor growth had a clientele that obviously didn't care about free Wi-Fi. And most probably, the guests had unlimited data plans. Maybe they were less price-conscious with their cell phone plans and features.

Gift Cards

Having the contact information of your clients is an important asset to your business. It is even more important than all of your high-tech equipment and technology in your restaurant. It is worth more than all of the fixtures and furnishings. You get my point.

A side benefit of having this database is that it is considered an asset. When you sell your restaurant in the future, the prospective buyer will be thrilled to know that you have marketing campaigns in place and a database for which the new buyer can reach out to. If everything is equal and a buyer is considering a restaurant to purchase, he or she will probably pick the restaurant with the database. You can even sell your restaurant at a premium when you have a substantial database. I would.

Remember, focus one is to constantly build your client base. Attrition is natural, and if you do not divert some of your attention to this important component of restaurant success, you will find yourself in a declining business. A business is either in one of two situations. It is either growing or declining. I challenge you to try to remember a situation when your business was not in either of these two states of operation.

This marketing strategy is to build your client base using gift cards. I like to use plastic gift cards that are pre-printed with the denomination (updated resources are found at www.SenseiOfSuccess.com). A popular denomination is $5. I also like to print a unique serial number on each card. The front of the card has my restaurant name. And the background of the card is printed in different colors. The big takeaway from adding these small details is that when the card is redeemed, I can track the origination of the marketing campaign that provided the card to the client.

The primary purpose of these gift cards is to capture the contact information of new clients. In other words, the client completes a form asking for their name, address, email, and other information. Then, the gift card is sent through the mail with an expiration date to urge the client to use it in a timely manner. I've known some businesses that ask for only the email. That does garner more responses from clients but leaves out the important information, such as address. To me, address is important because snail mail is still an important aspect of marketing. We'll cover more on that later.

I try to use the gift card in all aspects of my marketing. For example, the gift card form is found on my websites. In turn, there is signage in my restaurants stating receive a gift card by going to this or that website. It is used in my print ads. It is found in my newsletters. It is found on my business cards. The goal is to inform as many people as possible about the gift card giveaway.

Using a plastic gift card denotes value versus a paper coupon. When mailed, there is a certain bump impression in the mailing from the card. The envelope needs to be hand addressed. The envelope needs to have a real stamp. Every step of every campaign needs to be thought through the experience of the client. Think about all the mailings one receives. Time is scarce, and we sort through our mail quickly. Junk mail gets thrown away or placed in one pile. Another pile is reserved for mailings that should and do get opened. If it looks like a bill, personal mailings, or similar, it gets opened.

When a client receives the mailing, the tactile bump will lend curiosity, and the letter gets opened. Inside the mailing are the gift card and a nice letter informing the new client of your restaurant and benefits. The letter has important components that are covered in another chapter in this book called Copywriting 101.

It is very important to track your gift cards. You need to know which campaign the card originated from. You need to know how many cards were mailed out and how many were redeemed. I keep a spreadsheet tracking every card given to a client and redeemed. If, after a time, the card is not redeemed, another mailer is sent to remind them to redeem the card before the expiration.

The goal is that this campaign and every campaign you do must uphold its responsibility of paying for itself. Minimally, the campaign needs to break even. You and I don't have the money to throw into multiple campaigns and not see a return on investment. Tracking of this campaign includes the cost of postage, supplies, gift card printing, cost of transaction, and even the use of time to conduct and process.

And you cannot use the excuse that this marketing money is being used to build an image or branding. That is for huge corporations that do have the money to burn. These high paying advertisers aren't held accountable because there really is no way to attach traceability to advertising. Millions of dollars are spent to build an image or brand a product. But in the end, no one knows if the money helped to increase sales, do they?

We can't do that. Every dollar spent in marketing must return the same dollar. Ideally, we would like to see the return on investment be more than the original investment.

Groupon

Groupon and similar services sell gift certificates or vouchers on your behalf. The advantage of this, for your restaurant, is that Groupon has a huge marketing arm and is able to sell a lot of vouchers. Part of the attractiveness for clients is that the face value of the voucher is sold at a discount. For example, if Groupon sells a $30 voucher for your restaurant, the actual price to the client can be as low as $20. The client benefits from a $10 discount.

There is a downside besides the discount. If the $30 voucher is sold at $20, then the balance is shared between the restaurant and Groupon. The $20 balance could be a $10 payment for the restaurant. Notice I use the words "would" and "could." Terms are negotiable, but that basically is the gist.

The reason that this Focus 1 is mentioned in this book is because I can testify that it works. As mentioned before, Groupon has a big marketing engine and can sell a lot of vouchers in a relatively short time.

However, you need to be ready for the influx of clients. There could be times when your dining room is at full capacity, and it always seems that the Groupon holders come in at the same time. Food and service can be compromised. Many of the Groupon holders are first-time clients and experiencing this compromised food and service could mean the difference of them being a one-time visit versus a long-term relationship.

To really make this work, it is important that team members and the owner participate in full effort to capture names, addresses, and emails. If operations are really stressed and complaints are starting to emerge, a BOGO, bounce back, or similar should be ready to be given to help with the situation. Also, make it a priority to send a snail mail card for the Groupon redeemer thanking them for coming into your restaurant.

Only through testing and cost analysis will you determine if this works for you. It is worth trying. But I recommend implementing this strategy only when it is necessary to build your client list quickly.

Hotels

There are different reasons for marketing to hotels. The first reason is to invite hotel team members to come to your restaurant. You can offer a discount if they mention an employee discount code. Along the way, a relationship can be established in which catering could be part of your offerings (employee parties).

Focus One – Increasing Clients

But more importantly, you want to address your marketing to the guests at the hotel. Guests from out of town usually ask the team members of the hotel for recommendations on places to eat. This carries more weight than the technology reviews.

If working with the management, you might be able to get counter space to place your menu. The menu can have a card (postcard size) with a promotion and code. This code is for you to know where the promotion originated. Also, to entice the hotel to display your menus, you may offer a commission for each referral purchase.

The other aspect of hotel marketing is to get your restaurant in a display ad or page in the guest-room binder. This binder has the rules, code of conduct, and other information pertaining to the hotel operations. But usually, there is a section on places around the hotel such as services, points of interest, and restaurants.

You will be in competition with the other food services found in the binder, but if you offer an enticing promotion, that could be the tipping point for the guest to pick your restaurant for food ordering.

There is a slight downside to hotel marketing. Many of the guests are from out of town. Therefore, any promotion can't really account for the lifetime value of the customer. Instead, it's a one-time sale. Tough call as to whether you want to expend a lot of energy on making this work. Just run the numbers and analytics.

You can still capture the names and contact information and keep in a separate database. This database can still be utilized for client relationships. Along the way, you might want to find out if the guests are frequent travelers and come back to this hotel on a regular basis.

Landing Page

A landing page is typically a web page where internet users arrive. It is typically one page and above the fold. Above the fold is the area above the scroll area. In other words, if you need to scroll the page, everything under that area is considered below the fold.

What makes the landing page effective is that it only has one purpose. That one purpose is for the visitor to take action. And the user is not bombarded with distractions such as flashy gizmos and blinking lights that would otherwise divert their attention.

The landing page is used in many of the campaigns mentioned in this book. Whenever and wherever a client is asked to go anywhere on the internet to perform some form of action, the landing page is the place to go.

The elements of the landing page are important. But again, testing is still an important part of the analysis of the campaign. It should be kept simple. The headline at the top of the landing page should be no different from a direct mail letter. It is designed further to catch the attention of the client. You only have a moment to convince the visitor to stay and take action.

Also on the landing page should be some bullet points about the benefits the user will gain from taking action. There should also be testimonials (social proof) about what you do and offer. If you can use the first and last name of the people who gave the testimonies, it will make it more powerful.

There should be a phone number displayed. This seems counterintuitive, but there will be visitors coming from their mobile phones, and out of convenience, they would probably press dial and call versus trying to complete a form via the tiny screen of the cell phone.

However, there still needs to be a form. This is where testing is advised. The most effective form is when a visitor types in only an email address. But to build your database with detailed information, you may want to ask for complete information such as first and last name, address, city, state, zip code, phone number, and birthdate. The caveat is that every field that you ask the visitor to complete, the completion rate declines.

So you need to ask yourself what fields can be eliminated. If you can, leaving the zip code and state off because they are giving the city could eliminate some of the fields. The other suggestion is eliminating the city and state and keep the zip code.

Another helpful element is adding a picture or short video somewhere in the middle of the landing page to further catch the visitor's attention. Also adding an audio element further offers an additional way to deliver your message to act.

The takeaway is to have a separate landing page for each promotion and campaign. That way, you can track where the contact information came from and the source of the traffic to the landing page.

List Building and the Funnel

This is a short chapter because this important aspect of your marketing is repeated throughout this book. This important step in all your marketing is to capture the name, address, email, birthday, and phone number of every client that walks through your door. This even includes the client you may never see because he or she only receives takeout or deliveries from your restaurant.

One list is essential. However, it is recommended that you have multiple lists in different categories. These categories include repeat clients, business clients, cold clients, and catering clients. These lists help with tailoring specific marketing campaigns to the client.

Remember, when designing and implementing a campaign, always ask yourself how the contact information of the client can be captured. And then always keep the list up to date. More uses of your database is found throughout the book.

The next essential element of your marketing is to always have more than one marketing campaign working for focus one. You need to always be sending new clients to your business. There are many opportunities. The big marketing campaigns are found within this book. However, there are many more, and even more that haven't been created.

It is very easy to rely on just one source of name derivation. But what happens when something happens to the effectiveness of this campaign? Name building will become stagnant until you can get the next campaign going. This can take some time. Meanwhile, attrition starts to kick in and sales decline.

Businesses are either in two situations; it is either growing or declining.

Movie Theatres

Once you understand your perfect client and demographics, you will be able to pinpoint your advertising and marketing. A media that often gets overlooked but can play a part of your marketing strategies is to advertise in movie theatres.

When a movie is not being shown, there are ads displayed to the audience members. If there is a movie being shown that your ideal customer would watch, your advertisement will be more effective. For example, if you find that your ideal client likes to watch animations (you find out through your survey), then you can specify that your ad be shown in that bracket.

Chances are the audience members will be looking at their technology. You can utilize the moment by having the audience members participate in seeing your ad and then doing something with the technology.

For example, getting back to the free gift card promotion, you can offer a free gift card by going to a website or scanning a QR code. The audience member is taken to a special website page in which to request the gift card (see chapter for more details).

The takeaway is that you need to know that the customer walking through your door originated from the theatre advertisement. Then, you need to crunch the numbers and make sure that the ad dollar spent returns the same dollar in net sales. Analytics is important.

New Client

Many times, it is challenging to spot a new client. They may have found your restaurant by chance or a referral, or any number of reasons. Sometimes, there are cues from clients that they are new. For example, they might say that this is the first time here and recommendations. But outside of the cues, it is not good to offend an existing client by asking if they have been there before.

Team members are trained to look for cues. The goal is to get new clients onboard with offerings of the restaurant and come back soon. We want to make their visits habit and then keep the restaurant at the front of the line when it comes to a place to dine.

Therefore, I use several tools to help disclose the first-timers. The first tool is that every team member wears a button that reads, "If first time here, let me know." Then every so often, I will rotate table tents with promotions but also the phrase, "If first time here, let me know." The other cue is when a client brings in a promotion letter that team members know was sent to first timers (i.e. new movers, zip code lists, etc.).

Once the team member confirms the new clients, he or she will add in extra scripts about the restaurant and menu offerings, such as favorite dishes. Then later, the team member brings a packet. Within the packet is a contact form asking for their name, address, phone, and birthday. To help with giving all of this information, the team member informs that they will get a certificate for a gift on their birthday month. Also, a plastic gift card will be sent in the mail from our office (otherwise, they would ask for the card on the spot).

Within the next two days, the new client receives a thank you card and the plastic gift card. The client is added into the database, and from that day forward, they receive the monthly newsletter, birthday promotion, and other promotions throughout the life of the relationship.

Pay Per Click

Pay per click advertising is a simple strategy. It can get you results rather quickly. You can start to see results literally within a day. Pay per click advertising is when someone "clicks" on your advertisement. Then you are charged for the "click." The most popular pay per click advertising is found on search engines.

There is an upside and a downside to using this medium. The good news is that with pay per click, your ads are usually placed at the top of the searches. That is awesome because being listed first gets the views and, hopefully, a call to action. If you understand SEO (Search Engine Optimization), then you understand that it can take months before your restaurant gets listed in the search engine. And when it does, often, it gets listed far away from the first page. For now, remember the first-page listing is good. Everywhere else you get listed almost doesn't matter.

The other good news is that you can set your spending cap per day and even the region where the ad appears. You probably want your ad to show up in local searches versus another state. At all times, you know how much you are spending. You won't get shocked by this huge bill at the end of the month from advertising that can run twenty-four hours (even then, you can set when it's on).

You can test placement now by going to the most popular search engine. Then type in the style of your food and the location. For example, if you sell pizza in the city of Corona

California, you want to type in those keywords. Notice what is displayed. As of this writing, there is a good portion of the page dedicated to a map and paid ads. The natural listing is more toward the bottom. And chances are that those natural search results are listed at a handful before continuing on the next page.

Then, you want to think about how you search. If you are like most people, you read the first page and sometimes the second page. However, with most people, the third page is not read nor the subsequent pages. That is why it is very important that your business is listed on the first page.

Another upside is that you will have access to analytics. You will be able to see how and where the clicks were derived. You will be able to see when the clicks happened. It's just worth having a pay per click ad to access the powerful metrics that are available to you.

The downside is that pay per click offers limited ad space. Every word must earn its keep. Some words are restricted, such as "Free." Requirements and limitations are changing on a regular basis. This can make an effective campaign turn overnight, forcing you to rewrite or re-strategize.

Another downside is cost per keyword. When users type in a search term, the ads found at the top are determined by the words purchased by the advertiser. For example, if someone typed in the word "cat," the ads returned would be the ads which purchased the keyword "cat." The downside is that popular keywords have higher pricing. Some keywords can be a few cents. This can range up to tens of dollars per keyword.

The downside to keyword costs is that if you set a small cap per day for ad spending, you can reach your cap literally in one click if one of your keywords has a high cost. But the workaround is that you make a list of keywords. You will see how much each keyword costs. Then you need to make the executive decision whether to include the keyword(s) in your campaign.

As of this writing, cell phones are the resource for finding everything. That includes where to eat and what restaurant to go to. Therefore, the listings on the search engines on your cell phone are becoming an important resource for the public. In other words, your business needs to be listed on the mobile sphere.

And one of the quickest ways, again, is to participate in pay per click advertising. You are shortcutting your way into being listed. In other words, you need to get listed and paying for clicks; it's one of the quickest ways to achieve this goal.

Dynamic Calling

When implementing marketing campaigns, offering multiple options for clients to respond or act can be good or bad. The underlying takeaway for all campaigns is to test. Offering many options can confuse the client into not responding. On the other side of the coin, offering only one option can be the response that the client does not have access to or hinders their ability to act.

But one of the recommended response options to have on most, if not all, campaigns is a telephone number. Everyone is accustomed to seeing a phone number as a response mechanism. Even though the trend is of landlines becoming extinct in favor of cell phones, phone numbers are still important. Some mobile phones have the automatic capability to pop up a window whenever there is a phone listing to give the option of calling now.

But at the restaurant end, or any end, answering the phone is a pain. Asking a team member to log phone calls for tracking purposes is almost too much to ask for. They are already busy and multi-tasking.

Fortunately, there are phone services that can answer the phone and transcribe. That could be an option. Another option is there are phone services that answer robotically and can even transcribe. The data and analytics are possible.

But there is a higher-level phone service in which analytics and data is more detailed. It is called dynamic phone calling or dynamic phone dialing. For a monthly fee, you can create numbers that are unique for your marketing campaign. That way, you will know where the phone number was derived (please see resource chapter for recommendations).

The dashboard also shows how long the call was and when it was called. There is also information about who the caller is and the phone number (caller ID technology). The call can be forwarded to a human so that there is the dynamic sales script. Or the call can be recorded. And the companies can even transcribe the recordings.

Sometimes, clients are tentative to make a phone call, but it is the easiest option via mobile phones. If that is conveyed, you can also add the line twenty-four-hours, seven-days-a-week recorded line option.

Another powerful feature of the dynamic calling is the ability to track calls from pay per click advertising. You can set it up to integrate with the search engines and the analytics, and data on the dashboard will recognize the source.

Postcard Mailing

Postcards can be a viable solution to reducing direct mail costs. This is still a viable way to communicate with potential customers and even can be used for existing clients. The focus of the mailing is really limitless, but there seems to be some themes that permeate the mailings.

The popular theme is birthday mailings. Postcards can be printed in glossy colors, whereas envelopes tend not to be able to print with similarity. Picture yourself facing a stack of mail. You start sorting the mail over the trash can. The good pile is the important stuff, such as bills and correspondences that you consider important.

The mail and letters you don't care to read go into the trashcan. This includes sales flyers, catalogs, newspaper inserts, and cash advance letters. Many are advertising what you don't care about in that moment. However, when you come across a postcard with a detailed birthday cake or festive graphics, chances are that you will at least glance at it.

Therefore, it is important to catch the interest of the screener quickly or risk having your mailing become landfill. You can stack the odds in your favor. And the good news is that these elements are the same as the direct mail pieces you have learned throughout this book.

An element that should and must to be on your postcard is a headline. The headline needs to do what it is designed to do, which is get attention. It can be newsy, have the word free, be emotional, be humorous, or be serious. But, the headline needs to catch the attention of the reader, or it's in the round file.

The next element is a picture that coincides with the theme of the message. If you are promoting a birthday, maybe a glossy pic of candles, hats, cake, and ice cream may align with the theme? Maybe you are promoting your restaurant to new movers. A picture of your storefront, or a house, or a picture of the neighborhood?

Another suggestion is laden the postcard with testimonials. Social proof works, and when there are reviews that positively describe your business, a pain point on behalf of the client is reduced. It would be more powerful if you know certain questions that arise continuously. For example, maybe a question about having a happy hour arises on a regular basis. You can have a testimonial with that topic. The testimonial may state that you have plenty of festive offerings during happy hour and the service is outstanding.

Just like a direct mail letter, you need to include an offer. The offer needs to convey a short supply or limited time. In other words, you want a deadline in which the client acts now.

The call to action needs to be included. The client needs to be held by the hand and told what happens next. The client is to call now or go to the website. Maybe you want them to call. Or bring the postcard to the restaurant to redeem.

As far as promotion goes, you need to think about what will make the recipient take notice. It seems that promotions with a small percentage off don't really garner any eyeballs. Even the words "free" followed by "buy one, get one." There are times when this offer of BOGO (buy one get one) can work. If you have a gut feeling about using this one, just be sure to test.

You need to think over the top promotion. How about a free entrée or three-piece meal? Maybe offer a special off the menu dish? Maybe a dish and the team members will come to your table and sing a song? The creativity is limitless. Just think about how you can be outrageous. This can be done and still garner a ROI (Return on Investment).

If after testing you get mediocre results, meaning less than a dollar returned, you still need to give it a chance. An element that is overlooked is trying to sell from the postcard mailing. However, you can ease them into becoming a client. On the postcard, you can send the client to a landing page. From there, you can extend the copywriting to really engage and capture the client's attention. You might even be able to get contact information or make a sale.

Raffles

A raffle box is like the fishbowl concept. Where the fishbowl is directed toward businesses, the raffle is for families. I take the raffle box out for dinner and weekends. There is an entry form tucked into the check holder that dine-in guests are invited to complete.

This simple focus has many variables that you can test. For example, an option to offer the entry form online can be implemented. That could increase the sign-ups. But I prefer to offer only in my dining room to entice dine-ins. Prizes can vary as low as offering a free meal to products outside of your business category. For example, in the past, I have offered free tickets to the movies, amusement park, movie dinner package, and gift baskets.

It is important to note (as with any marketing effort) when obtaining sensitive information, such the guests' contact information, the form states that the information will be kept private. They also have the option to opt-out at any time.

There are some important points that will help with this promotion. First, I like to use a clear, plastic raffle box. This can be found on the internet. I keep some folded blank entry forms in the box. This is important immediately after a winner is picked. An empty box looks scary to the first entry dropper. Nothing attracts a crowd like a crowd.

Second, I have a chalkboard and like to post the winners every month. It gives the impression that I'm really giving away prizes and not just keeping the entry forms. The side benefit is that the winners like to see their names posted and openly brag about it (at least for a month). Many times, pictures end up on social media.

Third is awesome. Even though there is one winner of the raffle, I still make the rest of the participants winners. I reach out to them and explain that I'm sorry they didn't win first place. But there is an unannounced second place. Second place winners receive some sort of consolation. The second-place winner has no idea that everyone won second place. It still feels exclusive. I tend to mix it up with a free soft drink, discount, and anything that helps to bring the clients back into the restaurant.

Of course, you need to track everything. Make sure the prize that you offer makes sense to your marketing promotion. The prize can be as budgeted as low as offering a product from your restaurant or limitless in value. A dollar invested must return a dollar or more for every marketing effort.

Recorded Message

This strategy was mentioned a little in another chapter. But here, it is detailed in more depth. Free recorded messages should be a part of your marketing arsenal. There are different reasons to use this tool. At the very basic level, you can use recorded messages to give your location, hours, and website addresses. Clients call on a regular basis asking for this information. Team members then need to devote some time answering these questions. In a busy dinner rush, this can be a challenge with all the other multi-tasking that is going on.

But at the marketing level, free recorded messages are a non-intrusive way to deliver a message to your client. It is surprising to think that people will use the phone over accessing the internet in today's technological world. But the phone exists for a reason. People still use the phone.

You do not need to devote your phone line for the recorded message because that will stress resources. Instead, there are services that exist for this strategy. It is cost-effective, and if set up properly, a caller never receives a busy signal. A lot of the services offer an 800 number and/or vanity number that is easy to remember. This is important when people are driving in their car and see your marketing message on bandit signs (see chapter), window displays, or elsewhere.

Testing is required, but when someone calls the phone number, they can be taken to a menu where they press a number for hours, number for address, etc. However, this can be frustrating if they are calling to receive your marketing message.

The primary purpose to having a recorded message is that it's a low barrier for clients to receive a marketing message. If they know they are accessing a recorded message versus a live person, they will be more likely to do so. The recorded message should offer a call to action. For example, receiving a gift card by leaving contact information or mention a promotion code to receive a free appetizer or drink. Remember, you need to track the promotion.

There is another good reason to use these services. If you don't want to write down the addresses or replied messages, these services can also transcribe for you. You just receive an email with these messages transcribed. This is a great timesaver on your end.

Referral through Letterhead

There are different ways to bring new clients through the doors of your business. In this book, there are several marketing campaigns given to help with your goal. There are different levels of effectiveness. For example, a direct mail letter might be more effective than twirling a sign or a door hanging (see appropriate chapter). Again, only testing can verify what works for you.

One of the most effective ways to get new customers to your restaurant is word-of-mouth referral. Think back to a time when you yourself were looking for a place to eat. You would probably go to the restaurant your friends or family recommended versus reading a flyer on the wall.

Focus One – Increasing Clients

Word-of-mouth referral is probably the most effective type of referral campaign. One of the better campaigns to implement is to find a client that frequents your restaurant. Through time, you will be able to recognize your best clients and have a conversation with him or her.

Another way to center your focus on the best clients is to give a survey that asks how many times the client visits the restaurant in a month. Then, it's a matter of contacting the clients via their contact information.

The next step is to find out if they have or own a business. The reason is that you are trying to find the clients with a contact list database. When found, you take the letterhead of the company and craft a letter stating that the client goes to the restaurant on a constant basis. They are writing a long testimonial on their letterhead. The letterhead is important because it lends credibility.

The letter can state that the owner/client have arranged a special promotion. It would be best if the owner crafts the letter because it will have the tone and characteristics of the owner. But if the owner is not receptive to the idea, by all means, you can write it yourself.

Again, tracking is very important. Therefore, the letter needs to be brought to the restaurant to redeem. Or a special landing page and domain name may be used if working with the internet for marketing. Again, this campaign works better than the different referral systems. You need to test to confirm.

What was described is only one half of the process. The next half is to be really grateful for the referrals. You can reciprocate by creating a letter of referral yourself. After creating the referral letter on the behalf of the business owner, you send it out to your database of clients.

The caveat is that if you enrolled clients in your database with the stipulation that you will not sell, barter, or trade contacts, then you obviously need to abide by your promise. Then, you can balance out the favor by giving a food credit, gift certificates, or otherwise.

Schools

Chances are that there is a school nearby. Sponsoring a school team brings great benefits to you and your restaurant. First, you are helping the community and future generations that will lead us into the future. Second, this relationship can help with your goals for business growth and success.

Usually there are different levels of sponsoring a team. The more you donate, the more benefits go to your business. I like to sponsor at a level where I receive a plaque and opportunity to have my business card placed in the team program and media. The plaque hanging on the wall gives credibility to the restaurant that you are a supporter of the community.

With the business card, you don't want to have your business card placed in the media. Instead, you want to create an ad with a headline, offer, and a call to action. Remember that it needs to have a tracking code or something that will allow you to know the source of the inquiry.

You can also work with the school in other aspects. Around the end of each school term or semester, you can give gift certificates to the administration. The administration distributes the gift certificates as rewards to the students. You can pick students that have the best attendance, grades, or citizenship. Remember that when the student comes in to redeem, they will probably be with family. You need to capture (register) contact information.

You can also, with their permission, take a picture and use it for your website, the wall, or social media to highlight their achievement. This will also show support for the community. As a reminder, ensure that the gift certificate redeemer receives a bounce back or similar so that they come back. Minimally, a thank you card sent to them goes a long way toward them becoming a lifelong guest.

Educators have one of the most challenging careers (except for restaurant owners ☺). Sometimes, if your budget permits, do the free sack lunch campaign (see chapter). Or if you really can budget it, donate party trays to the school to thank the educators and administration for everything that they do. You are not being selfish by having flyers with a promotion and a call to action. And if the relationship solidifies, catering could be provided on a regular basis, but this time with compensation.

Website SEO

Here is a checkpoint. Do you have a website? If yes, good job, and read further for some tips on making it more effective. If not, after reading this chapter, put down this book and create a website. It surprises me tremendously how many of my competition does not have a website. The false perception is that a website is not needed. Social media takes the place of a website. Social media has its place (it has its own chapter), but the website is still king.

Focus One – Increasing Clients

Before, a long time ago, in a galaxy far away, one needed to code or hire a programmer to create a website. Today, you yourself can create a website in a matter of hours. In most cases, you can create a website for free. You can do that for the moment, but budget into your plans to pay for the hosting fee. Most free plans will throw ads onto your site, which basically conveys to the client you're low budget and unprofessional.

When choosing a company to use to build your website, make sure that there are several features offered. Since mobile phones are prevalent, make sure that when you build your website, it is automatically converted to the major formats (cell phone and computer). Make sure that the company offers an extensive library of templates. Many times, you are able to look through the templates. You can pay for templates that closely match your restaurant's image. But the free templates are such a good selling point, and I know there is a better chance it's compatible with the toolsets of the company.

Another feature you should look for is the toolsets offered. There should be an array of tools. They should be easy to use. Sometimes, you might need to sign up for a free account to try out these tools. If it is not intuitive, stop and sign up for another website company. There are many (you can check my website www.SenseiOfSuccess.com for resources).

Another mistake is to use the free domain provided by the web host. A web host is the company that "houses" your website on their computers and gives access to people who look for your website. The problem with using their free domain is that it is often a long address. It is hard to memorize and use in your marketing. And, like the free website, conveys a low budget and an unprofessional organization (your business).

Wi-Fi

Most everyone these days is connected to the internet. And with that said, most everyone has a cell phone. The most common observation in a restaurant's dining room is people looking at their cell phones. I myself subscribe to an unlimited data plan, but I do realize that it's kind of pricy compared to limited data plans.

Therefore, when a location offers free Wi-Fi, a number of people welcome this offering because they can turn off their connection and use the Wi-Fi to access the internet. I have some clients state that it was a hard decision to choose restaurants for dinner but chose my restaurant because I offered Wi-Fi.

I don't know if I should be offended because they didn't mention the choosing because of food or service. But Wi-Fi? The world is a peculiar place. The restaurant business is not exempt.

The easy way to offer free Wi-Fi is to give your clients your login information to your router. If you are doing that now, you may want to consider stopping this practice. The primary reason is that you yourself are probably accessing this login with your merchant account and even your online banking and other business stuff. Did you know that your private information, such as passwords and logins, can be hacked and viewed by those that have your Wi-Fi access information? It's true. Stop now.

But there are third-party companies that offer services and hardware that you may use in your restaurant to offer free Wi-Fi to your clients. But besides offering the free Wi-Fi, these services also capture information about each client that accesses your free Wi-Fi.

For example, a client completes a simple form at the beginning of the process. Then they are able to use your Wi-Fi throughout their dining time in your restaurant. The data captured by your hardware (provided by the third-party company) then sends the contact information through the internet to a database you access.

This database compiles a lot of good stuff about your clients. Through time, the database will provide information about repeat visits and demographics, such as age group, gender, and birthdays. Through these companies, you can also email promotions or correspondences to lost clients, repeat clients, and all clients.

You will also be able to see graphs and trends. This powerful information includes how many new clients come through your doors (is the marketing working). You will be able to see who and how many responded to your email promotions. The graphs give information about the percentage of clients who visit by frequency.

Even more powerful is that you can export the client information into your own primary database. You have a database, right? Remember that you are building an asset. These names add value to your restaurant, just like the furniture and fixtures.

As mentioned, there are multiple companies that offer similar but different services regarding offering Wi-Fi to your clients. As mentioned before, please check the resource page in the back of the book to access the latest recommended companies.

Multi-Step Business Card – Dessert, Appetizer, Entrée

This is a good promotion in which the team members at the front of the house get involved. This can be a little tricky. If the team member is not onboard, the promotion will not be effective.

There is a script involved. The waitress and waiter need to ask the guests if it is the first time visiting. If not, then the conversation can turn to the menu and specials. However, if it is the first time, then the underlying goal is for them to come back several more times so that the dining option of your restaurant becomes a habit.

The team member needs to remember that it is their first time. Then, at the end of the meal, the guest is asked if they would like dessert. If they say they are full, then the team member says that it is okay, but then tell about how good the dessert is. Then the team member writes on a special card stating that the next time they come in to dine, then the dessert is free.

When the guest comes back the next time to redeem the card, then they proceed with the meal and free dessert. At the end of the meal, the team member states that the guest did not have an appetizer. The appetizers are awesome, and they need to try the house special appetizer. Then the team member takes out another card and handwrites a free note for a free appetizer at the next visit.

The third visit, the guest may only have the appetizer and a drink. It is okay. The team member then writes another card for a free entrée. The caveat is that the comps need to be tested for return on the dollar. If the chain of dessert, appetizer, and entrée does not work well, then you can mix it up with appetizer, dessert, entrée, or drink.

This is a good program to implement if you have the team members actively participating. They may resist at first but will most likely find that the tips increase. The guest feels that the team member helped him or her out and will reciprocate with a higher tip for the favor.

It is easy to track. When a team member receives a card with dessert, then they know that it is the guest's second visit. The team member will then know the next sequence is appetizer. On your end, the team member collects the card and gives them to you. You can then track the promotion.

This promotion can be gamed in that the guest can say that it is their first time every time they come in. Then over time, they have a collection of cards. You can offset the cheating by having the customer fill out the card with contact information. Then the team member can look into a database to see if this is a repetition.

But it does entail more work for the server. You just need to take it step by step and ease into the extra safeguards as they start to get out of hand. However, you will come to find out that this gaming is really minimal.

Focus Two – Increasing Sales per Transaction

Hungry customers have seen your advertisements and marketing campaigns from the first section, and now that they know your restaurant exists, you want to encourage them to spend more. Increasing your customer base and increasing the amount they spend are the only ways to increase your sales, so figuring out how to keep them coming back and spending more on appetizers, desserts, and other "extras" will boost your bottom line.

Package Insert Program

The Package Insert Program, or PIP, takes the opportunity of delivery and take-out. Whenever a client orders from one of the two, a sheet of paper is included with the packaged order. The sheet can be an 8.5-by-11-inch or cut in half.

The opportunities for this are varied. On the sheet can be a bounce-back coupon. This can be tracked by having the client bring it with them on their next visit. Or there can be a special code that can be utilized online to print a coupon. This is tracked by having the client type in their email and a coupon is emailed back.

Focus Two – Increasing Sales per Transaction

The cost to this program is the printing. But there is a way to implement this program for free. I usually use an 8.5-by-11-inch printed insert. The front side is dedicated to my restaurant. However, the back side is reserved for other non-competing businesses and services.

The page can be divided up into eighth-inch chunks. The business can give you a business card or artwork. I'm really challenged in the graphic arts area and just simply paste their artwork onto the page. I take my printing costs and divide the cost eight ways.

The benefit is that these businesses, if the offer is attractive enough, will start to get clients coming to them automatically. By having your restaurant deliver these promotions for other businesses, you are using your name as an authority to refer.

This partnership with businesses can include many categories. For example, I have martial arts studios, massage services, nail salons, hair salons, an optometrist, and phone repair on my roster. I think if you do a little pondering, you can do the same.

Package inserts do get read. To increase readability, you will want to change it on a semi-regular basis. Good opportunities include the holidays and special occasions. There should be a small note thanking the client for the order, and if there are any issues, please contact immediately.

Art Gallery

I like this marketing weapon because it offers some great benefits to your restaurant, your clients, and the community. Even though it is listed as a focus two, it can easily be labeled as a focus one or three. This marketing campaign entails displaying original artwork of artists in your community.

The primary benefit is that it offers a new income stream. The walls are now paying for your operations, along with the floors. When a painting sells, you get a commission that is previously negotiated by the artist.

Since the artwork is original, the artist will be sending clients to you via flyers, internet, and word of mouth. The artwork also keeps your dining room fresh looking by having paintings rotated on a constant basis (through sales and non-sales).

Another benefit is that the artist can be the subject of your newsletter and website (remember original content and SEO). You can also interview the artist(s) and showcase them on a video within your channel and website.

There are some tips that can help to make this campaign effective. First, it makes sense to talk with the artist about your food category, décor, and your guest demographics. If your guests have pets, then maybe artwork based on animals might help with selling. If your guests like traveling, maybe artwork based on exotic locales might work well.

Artists can be found everywhere. There are hobbyists, art students from the local university, and artists that are professional. Another great source is the local art association. Art associations are found in every city. You can work with the association and plan out a beneficial arrangement for both parties.

Working with an art association also has benefits. You can arrange to have a meeting in your restaurant and offer a special dining package. You can find an artist that will offer a paint-and-dine on your slow night. This paint-and-dine comes in various shapes and forms. But the big takeaway is that guests (from your list) are invited to dine and, at the end of the evening, walk away with a self-created painting. The guests pay for a special paint-and-dine package. It becomes a great social gathering and most everyone walks away with amazement for creating their own artwork.

Another benefit with working with an endeavor such as your art association and artists is that it helps with your rankings with search engines. You can work with the association and artists by trading links to each other's websites. It is almost assured that the association and each artist have a website. By them linking to your website and vice versa, the credibility of an art association gives your website credibility. Search engines like this and push your rankings higher. There is more information about this in another chapter on internet marketing.

Always keep in mind the marketing that you learned throughout this book. If you can have art association meetings in your restaurant, capture the contact information and entice them with a gift card or promotion that will bring them back. Any student that comes to the dine-and-paint should be added to a special list. This list can be used to inform guests of future painting parties.

Pricing

One of the fastest and quickest ways to increase ticket sales? Raise your prices. This is one of the hardest ideas to grasp because we restaurant owners are aware of the pricing of our competition.

Focus Two – Increasing Sales per Transaction

We fear raising our prices and then losing customers in droves. Yes, you might lose some of the price-conscious customers. However, you will find that clients do stay because of reasons other than pricing.

Remember, with all things being equal between you and a competitor, the client will most likely choose pricing as the tipping point. But also remember that you are unique through the WMYU (see chapter) so that a client cannot compare you to another competitor.

By the way, your WMYU cannot be that you have the lowest prices. Then it will become a pricing war. There will always be the new restaurant down the street that looks at your prices and then proceeds to price their items lower. You can't win. We are mom and pops. We cannot compete with the chains and big box companies.

Now that we have price wars out of the way, ask yourself when do you raise prices? I know of restaurants that raise their prices yearly. And this is almost by necessity. In my area, I've seen utilities, COGS, repairs, and overhead rise every year. Why shouldn't my prices?

To tell you the truth, the customers that do leave the restaurant because of pricing always seem to be the picky customers who complain about every little detail. I have a policy to cater to everyone. But to tell you the truth, these price-conscious customers leaving is really not a stress point for me.

Try raising your prices a few percentage points. If you do experience a dramatic decline in sales, you can always revert and send a message to your client list with an apology. But I have yet to meet or learn of a restaurant that needed to revert back to original pricing.

Focus Three – Increasing Repeat Customers

You've encouraged your customers to come inside and order more than they most likely originally thought, so how do you get them to come back a second, third, or fourth time? How do you turn your establishment into their regular eatery?

Birthdays

There are reasons why you want to acknowledge a client's birthday and invite him or her to celebrate this occasion in your restaurant. Birthdays are rarely celebrated alone. Usually, diners that come to celebrate birthdays minimally come in pairs and up to groups. And even if coming as a pair, the ticket spent is normally higher. Birthday celebrators tend to add on appetizers, desserts, and drinks.

It's very important when you captured their name and address and other contact information that you also ask for their birthday. Just know that people are sensitive about giving information such as their birthdate. But you can state that the month and day is all that is needed. But leave a field for the year. You will find that there will be several clients that will give the year.

Focus Three – Increasing Repeat Customers

This one piece of information, the year, is important. If you set up your database completely, you will be able to see a trend with age groups. And through time, you will be able to cite your ideal customer. The ideal customer can then direct your thinking as to how to create marketing campaigns and advertisements. You want to speak the language, thinking, desires, and fears of your ideal customer.

Once you have captured the birthdate of your clients, send a month-ahead email and snail mail a postcard wishing them a happy birthday, and invite the client to bring friends to celebrate this special occasion in your restaurant. The important inclusion in the correspondence is that they will get a free entrée with no strings attached. They just need to dine in to claim the free entrée. It is true that some individuals will come in by themselves and just get the entrée with a glass of water. However, I can only count on my one hand these occurrences. And then I feel sad that they came in by themselves to eat alone.

But you will find that the majority of claimants will indeed spend more, and the numbers that are returned are satisfactory enough to overcome the free entrée. You can also limit the entrée by placing a value. For example, the free entrée covers 70 percent of your entrée offerings. However, if the client picks an expensive entrée, then he or she is asked to pay for the difference after the limit.

Birthday promotions are really nothing new. Chances are that another business (your competitor) may be offering another promotion to the same client in the same month. It is important how you can make your experience more memorable, and even more, social-media memorable.

When a client comes in to redeem their coupon, at the end of the meal, they get a birthday song from the team members. The birthday client also gets a free t-shirt (with the restaurant name) or similar gift that is not food related. Then several days later, a real birthday card is sent to the client saying thank you for choosing us to celebrate this special occasion, and we really enjoyed this festive occasion. Also, within the thank you card is another coupon or bounce-back promotion inviting the client to come back soon (deadline on coupon).

The caveat is that you must be careful with promotions and coupons. Be mindful and careful. Each restaurant and each owner's purpose are different. But you must consider each step and marketing campaign you use. Each pathway can affect a business positively or negatively in the minds of the clients.

A great example of this scenario is JC Penney. At one time, JC Penney was a coupon and sales machine. It seemed like there were sales, promotions, and discounts daily. Then things started to decline (sales). A new CEO came in and immediately stopped the sales and discounts. He wanted to create a shopping experience of fixed pricing and enjoyment. Soon afterward, sales and related profits dropped in half. It seemed that the customers shopped at JC Penney because they enjoyed trying to find the best deals and sales in the store. It was challenging to rid the perceptions that were already in the minds of the shopper.

Returning Clients
Making the Restaurant Child-friendly

This is a tough call. I realize that there are some restaurants that would be okay with not having families step into their dining rooms with young children. One of the headaches is cleaning up, because oftentimes, food finds its way to the floor. Or babies start crying or yelling, which definitely affects the experience.

However, if you have a reputation as being a child-friendly restaurant, that leaves more opportunities for the family to come back. With that said, there is increased spending and repeat visits.

There is some marketing that can be done with families with children. The little touches make a great impression with the parents. A special menu can be created for the children. Specially printed placemats with coloring opportunities and puzzles can be displayed.

Games can be created to get the children involved. One of the hardest parts for a parent is waiting for the food after ordering because the children are getting impatient. One of the fun games is to place objects around the dining room and have the children try to find the objects with the rule that they need to stay in their seat and just point rather than yell out. Miniature fish can be placed on shelves and different places in the room. The children are told that there are fifteen fish placed around the room, and they are to find Nemo's friends, who seem to have gotten lost. If all fifteen fish are found, the child gets a free dessert.

Another marketing campaign is to issue a special printed currency that is given to each child and for each visit. The currency should be serial numbered and/or printed in such a way to reduce counterfeiting.

When the child and parents find out that this currency can be redeemed for prizes, they find their way back to the restaurant more times than ever.

Picture what is happening when a family is in a car and deciding on a place to eat. The children know they are closer to redeeming a prize and will be vocal about going to your restaurant to earn the extra currency.

Another variable that can be thrown in this campaign is to dedicate a place in the dining room showcasing the prizes. Remember, you are tracking each currency with a serial number and are able to determine the profit margins from what the family spends. Prizes can be eye openers with bikes, video consoles, apparel, and more. If you are at a loss of what prizes to get, you can issue a survey to your clients asking what they would like to see as prizes. Parents know because their children are asking on a regular basis.

Newsletters

It is necessary to always keep in communication with your existing clients. We live in a world with many distractions. It's very easy to be in some sort of habit. For example, I think everybody who dines out has a favorite or regular restaurant. But someday, another restaurant garners your attention through some awesome promotion, recommendation from a friend, or something else. Then, your regular or favorite restaurant gets forgotten. Possibly. Most likely.

I myself can think of recent examples where I stopped going to my favorite restaurant. One restaurant I was going to once a week after my restaurant closed for the night (this favorite restaurant was open twenty-four hours). This was a regular happening for at least a couple of years. I would go there to eat different food, work on my papers, and basically to de-stress. Then I went on vacation, and when I came back, I stopped going to the restaurant. No real reason. Just stopped.

One of the important tools to keep that relationship with your client base is using newsletters. There are two options. Preferably, sending a newsletter in the mail is the best. However, postage and printing can be costly. It is through tracking and cost analysis that you will be able to determine if it's viable. A popular format is one color ink ad on 8.5-by-17-inch size paper. The newsletter is folded, and bulk rate postage is used to reduce mailing costs.

A way to defray costs is to have inserts or ad placement of non-competing businesses. The non-competing businesses pay for part of the mailing to have their flyers or ads in the newsletters. If done correctly, clients see it as helpful rather than shameless promotions. Complementary businesses are numerous. Think of plumbers, martial art schools, salons, carpet cleaners, cell phone repair, and pet groomers.

The other option is through the internet. You can create your newsletter digitally and then send it with the push of a button. However, the downside is that you need to be careful with SPAM laws. You can reduce this issue by using several services that adhere to the emailing laws. You simply create your newsletter and send through their system. The other benefit is that these services offer stats, such as newsletters sent, open rate, bounce rate, and cancel rates (service providers are listed behind book and updated on website).

Focus Three – Increasing Repeat Customers

The important takeaway from newsletters is that it cannot be a promotion fest. Clients get tired of seeing constant promotions from your business. Newsletters can be entertaining, informative, and useful. However, there should be some promotion or action on the client's part so that you are able to track the success of the send outs. Again, metrics is important. Every dollar spent should garner a return of a dollar or more.

If you are challenged by writing a newsletter, there are article databases found on the internet. These services offer articles that can be used—often for free. The stipulation is that you also credit the author and include the link found in the author resource box. Often, the link leads the client to another website that promotes something that might not be in alliance with your business. You will need to decide if it makes sense for you and your business.

Another resource for content for your newsletter is through any of the various internet services that offer freelancing. You can hire a writer to create content. The good news is that the content is unique and can be re-used for your website, social media, print, etc. A side note is that if you use unique content for your website, you can increase the likelihood of being listed higher in the search rankings. This is the butterfly effect at its best.

There is a metric that for every month you are not in contact with your clients, you lose 10 percent of the client base. If this holds true, in ten months, if you are not communicating with your clients, you lose all your patrons to another business or competitor. Therefore, it is important that the newsletter is part of your marketing arsenal. If it's really challenging to send out a newsletter every month, at least quarterly is better than nothing. At once a year, I'm not sure if it's beneficial.

Partnership Program

If you start the package insert program (see appropriate chapter), you will have a list of businesses that you have partnered with to help each other out. This marketing program is also used to help both entities.

Whenever a dine-in guest spends a certain amount (for me, $100), they get a voucher or gift card from one of my "partners." This voucher is usually for a free trial or subscription for their program and/or services. Some of the partners on my list include a martial art studio, an indoor playground facility, a dance studio, and a massage service.

The $100 sale helps the restaurant because it increases the ticket sale. The purchase also helps the partner because they "automatically" get an interested guest into their door. Then, through multiple visits, the guest becomes an enrolled client. The relationship is built through the free trial. However, it is important that the partner obtains contact information and performs the same style of marketing as you just learned.

Some proprietors balk at offering free trials, but there are some considerations that offering this promotion makes sense. They are already paying for overhead, whether it is one client within your door or one hundred. Therefore, offering a free trial does not contribute more to the costs already associated with their business.

Marketing is a time constraint for a business owner. Unless you're paying for someone who is dedicated to marketing, you're usually the person that does the marketing. This marketing promotion lets you send clients to them, saving time and energy for customer acquisition.

There are benefits to the partner that they wouldn't consider unless you enlighten them. Clients are already pre-screened with spending. They have proven it by spending $100 in your restaurant (or you and your partner can determine a beneficial sale price that makes sense for both endeavors). Client acquisition cost is minimal. After the end of the free trial or service, clients pay for the subscription, renew, and add lifelong value to your partner's establishment—remember, clients walk into their door automatically.

To further entice the partnership, I offer counter space in my restaurant where the partnering business may place flyers, promotions, or any other advertisement that makes sense. Sometimes, I allow a raffle box. I also offer free advertising space in my Package Insert Program (see appropriate chapter). And if the delivery or take-out order is at $100 or over, I drop in the gift card along with a welcome letter to the free trial and/or service.

Rewards Program

Rewards programs are the components of a business that give bonuses for clients who come back on a regular basis. We humans like to acquire and get rewarded. With rewards programs, both aspects are addressed.

Clients that purchase typically receive one point per dollar spent. Then, as the points accumulate, it can then be used toward purchases. If the balance is high enough, a client can receive a free meal. Another reward type is each guest gets a stamp or card punched per visit. After a certain number of visits or purchases (punches), the client receives a freebie or discount.

It is highly recommended to go with third-party services. This is such an in-depth, detailed endeavor you could find yourself immersed with most of your precious time devoted to this area of marketing. Unless you go with the punch-card system, go with a third-party service. Please see the resource page and website for updated recommendations.

Another reason for going with a third-party service is that many of them have portals with data access. This is powerful stuff. Because you will not only be able to see your client list of enrollees but you will be able to access some great information too. For example, you will be able to see who your best clients are, how many times they visit your restaurant, and ticket price.

This data will help you home in on your best, ideal client. You can conduct a special survey that asks for information such as hobbies, travels, likes, dislikes, suggestions, and the list goes on. Of course, they should be compensated for the completion of the survey. The information mined from these guests is gold. You can then narrow down your marketing to your ideal guest. This will make guest cost acquisition more effective and profitable. You will know the average ticket price and frequency of visits. I'm smiling as I write this.

Voice Broadcast

Voice broadcast is another phone-based technology that seems to escape the marketer's focus arsenal. We assume that no one uses the phone anymore. But that's not true. Voice broadcast helps with focus three where we want to have our guests come back to our restaurants on a regular basis.

One of the powerful ways of keeping us in mind is to have regular communication with our clients. Voice broadcast uses technology in which every guest receives a phone call from you. But you don't call every phone number. There are calling services that do the calling. It is not a live person but rather your recorded voice (more effective if it's your voice—authority marketing). With the technology and sophisticated recording equipment, the recording sounds like a live person.

This isn't spamming because you already got permission to contact your guest. Right? Make sure to have the fine print read that their information will not be bartered, sold, or given away. And that from time to time they will be reached out through newsletter, email, or phone but can opt out at any time.

As with the other marketing weapons in this book, there are some tips to make it more effective. When you set up voice broadcast, make sure to pick the option of delivering the message only if the receiver does not answer the phone. If they do answer the phone, they will have the opportunity to ask questions. But it's really hard to answer questions when it's a recording. Then your credibility will be shot.

Another tip is not to make all your voice broadcasts a promotion fest. You are keeping a relationship. Your guests are your family. Make sure that a chunk of your messages is to wish them a happy holiday or similar greeting. If you set it up correctly, you can even have the message wish them a happy birthday.

Some people don't even receive phone calls from their immediate families regarding birthdays or happy holidays. A lot of times, these days, it's a text. Really sad how society and technology affect each other.

Section Two – Miscellaneous Restaurant Toolsets – Strategies/Tactics

Many of the marketing suggestions and strategies I previously mentioned in section one were geared specifically to getting customers in the door, having them purchase more, and having them come back at a later date. In this section, we're going to take a look at some of the tactics and strategies I've used in the past with great success, as well as strategies I know many restaurateurs are missing. While they may not seem important, these toolsets can be what make or break your business.

Marketing nuggets are short chunks of marketing for your restaurant. Not meant to be time-consuming but just takes a small chunk of your marketing agenda. Not really considered a campaign. Although one can make a case that it fits in the overall campaign that involves the three focuses.

Online Table Reservations – Search Engine Aspect More Exposure, Impression Of Popularity, Social Proof

Online table reservation service is conducted through a third-party entity. If you consider yourself too small for online reservations, you might want to reconsider. There are advantages, and it pertains to the theme of this book.

As it states, online reservations allow clients to hold a table at a certain time and a certain date. More and more clients are favoring restaurants that offer online reservations because, essentially, there are no surprises.

Reflect on your own situation. There are peak times and days. The busy days include Valentine's Day and Mother's Day. Did you get a lot of calls for reservations? Have you received comments and questions regarding wait times? Have you had clients see a crowded dining room and then turn around to go to their second choice? Not sure of the answer? Rest assured that these are common questions from restaurants that don't offer online reservations.

With online reservations, clients can rest comfortably knowing that they have tables when they arrive. If they are on the road, making reservations is even more important because they wouldn't want to drive to your restaurant and find that they must wait or not have a table at all.

There are now apps for mobile phones in which clients can book reservations. This gives the impression that your restaurant is an established, technology-savvy business. The millennial generation favors technology and will nod approval toward doing business with you.

For your teams, they will be able to forecast and anticipate table fills and prep accordingly. Staffing can be adjusted if prior knowledge of table fills is known. The back of the house can also benefit with this information by increasing or decreasing prep stock and processes accordingly.

As a marketing tool, you can get a jump on the reservations. You can see who reserved and then cross check with client information, such as favorite dishes and food allergies. You can even spot your best customers and amaze them with something special. A handwritten thank you card sitting on the table can go a long way for the client to be enchanted. Or a flower and a piece of chocolate presented on a serving dish makes for another amazing moment.

If you see that the dining room is running a little light, you can send a text blast or email with a message about a dine-in special that can only be redeemed at a particular hour which coincides with your light time slot.

Website Format

Other components that should find their way onto your website will help you track the effectiveness of the website and act as a funnel to bring you new clients. Web forms are easy to implement via the hosting company's toolsets. These web forms should include a form to sign up for a gift card (as mentioned in another chapter). Remember that the response of the signer is that this is the internet, and why would they need to provide full contact information?

My response is that a real gift card is being sent in the mail and address is obviously important. However, you may choose to just have the signer include an email rather than the full contact information. I know marketers who take this route and do very well. Then, in following correspondences, the marketers ask for the full contact information when the clients are more comfortable with the business.

Another component you need to add to your website is the form to sign up for your newsletter. There is good news here. When you work with an online emailer, oftentimes, they will have a form creator. This form can then be added to your website. When a client subscribes to your newsletter, the contact information is automatically placed into the newsletter database. You do not need to take the form information and then add it into a database list. It's done automatically.

To further aid with tracking and metrics, Google offers a tool called Analytics. All you need to do is add a provided script into your website. Then you access your Google account and the Analytic site will provide some really good information, such as origin of visitor, time, what search term, and so much more. It gets me excited just thinking about how powerful this tool is. And I am even more excited that my competitors don't even know about this powerful marketing weapon.

Another hack with websites is that delivery through third-party services is sweeping the country. They make money by taking a commission. But the tradeoff is that they spend a lot on marketing, and your restaurant does get orders. A huge downside is that customers go to the third-party portal. This is bad because on that portal is a smorgasbord of options. The customer can pick from many categories. They also can order from your competitor. There is no exclusivity.

That is why I've created my own websites for delivery. Through SEO and giving my clients the web address, there is a little more exclusivity. On the website are links to the third-party delivery. The clients are taken around the portal and lead directly to my menu options.

As mentioned before, I have my delivery website posted on the walls, my menus, flyers, and any other marketing campaigns I may have going. You have learned that websites and domain names are cheap. Start building.

Website Format

TRACKING WEB FORMS, NEWSLETTER, SIGN-UP MENU, HOURS ETC. SEPARATE WEBSITE FOR ORDERING DELIVERY

SEO – Search Engine Optimization

Before getting into the nitty-gritty of websites and domain names, Search Engine Optimization (SEO) needs to be discussed. SEO is a huge in-depth topic in itself and can take its own thick book. SEO pros make six figures a year just keeping on top of this topic and implementing it for companies. The takeaway about SEO is that whenever someone searches for a topic on the big search engines, the goal is to have your company appear in the top three to five rankings of that search.

Think about your search habits. If you search, like most of the population, we input a search term or keyword and then the results are returned. We peruse the first page. Very rarely do we explore beyond that first page. Many times, we do not go past the top five. By the way, this top area is considered "above the fold." Akin to the newspaper that has a fold in the middle, "above the fold" refers to the area on the viewing screen without having to scroll down further.

If you want to devote time with SEO, you will find that it's a fascinating subject. It's really satisfying to see your website climb in rankings and eventually get to the top of the fold. It's sort of like free advertising. Hundreds and thousands of people will have the chance to see your restaurant without you having to spend a dime. But that dime is traded for time.

Please know that algorithms for rankings do change and have changed. In the recent past, businesses that were making tons of money being ranked number one in the searches literally saw their income streams hit a wall and stop when their ranking disappeared.

Therefore, don't take it too seriously to be ranked number one. But fortunately, there are some steps you can take to help you stay on the first-page rankings. Put yourself as the client. When someone is searching for your type of restaurant, I would input the search terms "type of food, city" or "type of food, near me." Search engines place some credibility on domain names with the keywords within.

For example, if you have a pizza restaurant named Roma's Pizza in the city of Riverside, think about how people may search for your restaurant and even your category. I would type in "pizza near me," or if I knew of your restaurant but didn't know where you were located or the hours, I would type "Roma's pizza Riverside." That is the domain you should register. Also, it is not against the law to have more than one domain pointing to your website. With this example, you would register www.RomasPizzaRiverside.com and www.PizzaRestaurantRiverside.com. The search engines will like you.

If you can get other website entities to link back to you, the search engines feel that you are important enough to link back. This is a little tougher and can take time. But if you have a rather large circle of influence, linking to and linking back to you is powerfully effective. The best link back is from an organization or entity like the government or educational institution. But that is challenging and futile at best. However, if you somehow have a relationship with a school with catering, then a link from them (backlink) is possible. Other ideas for backlinks include your distributors, possibly your local Chamber of Commerce, vendors (tell them you will do business with them if they link their website to yours :/), and partners through your partnership program (see appropriate chapter).

The other component to help with SEO is to add content. Besides the pretty pictures of your food and restaurant, you need to add content that is original and is laced with the keywords that people use to search for your category and restaurant. The content should be added on a regular basis. Writing is challenging and time-consuming, but the good news is that you are working on newsletters, right (see appropriate chapter)?

It takes time for a website to climb in rankings. A search engine considers new sites as non-established. The sites that have been around a long time are considered seasoned and get the nod to higher rankings if everything else is equal. That is why it's very important to establish your website now.

PBS – Public Broadcasting Station – Underwriting

It's an exciting feeling when a winning advertising and marketing campaign breaks even or even returns more than the initial cost. At that point, different media gets explored. Television, radio, newspapers, and cable come to mind.

But there is a little-known channel that doesn't get considered. That is the local Public Broadcast Station (PBS). At first glance, PBS doesn't accept advertisements. And on paper, that is true. But that policy is in the past.

Today, the policy has changed. On the surface, the spot looks like advertising. However, the key term is called underwriting. And if you pay close attention, there are times when a spot comes on and there is verbiage about the show was underwritten by "company name."

There is also good news. Rates tend to be affordable for restaurants. Depending on the area, you could be looking at rates hundreds of dollars below similar media, such as local network spots and even cable.

Stations also have studios in which to create your spot for a nominal fee. If that is the route you take, you can also request the spot video and re-purpose it in many ways. You can park it on a video sharing site. You can use it on your website. You can play it on social media.

It is very tempting to cross over to the dark side of marketing. And if you haven't already guessed, branding is the least important of your goal of profit growth in your business. We are all inclined to just follow what we have seen in the past on network television. The big companies pay tons of money to ad agencies whose job is to make us feel good about the product. Then the narrative is that if we feel good about a product or harbor some emotion, then when we take action to purchase, we would choose the product versus the competition.

But the reality is we don't have the funds to build branding. It would take years and deep pockets to even touch the same levels as the big companies. Remember, our goal is to focus on returning every dollar that we spend. If it breaks even, it's okay. But the real goal is to turn a profit on our marketing dollars.

Some of the key points are that we want the viewer to take action and also convey a deadline. Minimally, the spot should convey a scarcity, such as limited supply. The caveat is that PBS might have restrictions on promotions. But you can still reduce the salesmanship. Another way is to have the viewer call a phone number. Rather than you having to answer the phone, you can use a third-party answering service to complete the calls. They can transcribe the message also.

PBS has a big lineup of shows that cover the spectrum of information and entertainment. Even though we come from a restaurant and food standpoint, you might also want to test spots for travel shows, financial, serials, etc.

Since we are on the subject of PBS, you can offer your services for catering and delivery. You can have a subscription service in which the station commits to catering packages at reduced cost. Or another way to create a relationship with the station is to have your team members volunteer during the fundraisers where they answer phones. If the station allows, your team members can wear t-shirts with the business name.

Another takeaway is that each station is different. You may come across a station that is stricter on their policies. But with the current state of public funding, stations are more receptive to working with underwriters.

Gift Certificates

Gift certificates should be a part of every restaurant's offering. There are different forms of gift certificates. One can consider the gift card marketing mentioned throughout this book as a gift certificate. Other restaurants use a postcard printed with gift certificate wording. Other businesses do use a credit-card-type format.

But I like to use the paper gift certificates. It's more for preference. There are companies that sell blank certificates that can be printed through a printer (ink or laser). I like these because there are security components on the gift certificates. These include holograms, thermal inks, microprinting. And the paper feels like a higher quality (similar to currency).

Also, the gift certificate can be custom printed with links to landing pages to enroll in programs such as the birthday club, rewards club, and newsletter subscription. It's another way to get the message out about your different offerings.

There are some side benefits to gift certificates. The biggest benefit is that gift certificates do not get redeemed. A log is kept, and every year, there are gift certificates that are categorized as

Gift Certificates

MIA. I wish I could tell you the reason. My best guess is that the gift certificate gets lost. Or the recipient user forgets about redeeming.

Gift certificates get sold throughout the year. However, during the holiday season, that is the high season. It just takes a little push through the newsletter or an email blast. Signage throughout the restaurant also helps to remind clients of gift card offerings.

Other ways of increasing per purchase sales is offering a discount on the face value. For example, buy five certificates and get a discount of $3. On your end, it's a great way to get additional cash flow quickly without taking the immediate hit of COGS.

There is a caveat. You need to investigate the gift certificate laws. But if accepted, credit card purchases of gift certificates are more prevalent than cash. This is mostly because clients are using their rewards credit cards to purchase gift certificates, which gets them points or air miles. But the downside to this is that your merchant account takes fees, such as percentage and swipe. Essentially, you are losing on the sale.

But the other side of the coin, they would have used the credit card in your restaurant, and you would have lost out on the fees anyways. You would need to monitor and agree to credit cards if it makes sense.

USP – WMYU – What Makes You Unique

Picture yourself in the shoes of your client. Ask yourself, what is the reason you would dine at your restaurant? Are there other options? Are there competitors that can fulfill the same desire or option? Would it also suffice just to do nothing? Tough questions. When I asked myself those questions, I was stumped. The next question I asked myself was why I was in the restaurant business.

Notice that this chapter does not have a focus. This is really an important question and answer. Get this correct, and the profits reaped from your marketing efforts will be so much easier. Get this wrong, and your marketing will still work. It just won't be as dramatic and maybe even more frustrating and challenging.

What Makes You Unique (WMYU) is addressed toward your business. There are different terms out in the marketing world, but I feel that the owner is the extension of the business and vice versa. What makes you unique is what makes the offering of the restaurant unique.

So go ahead. Look at the first paragraph and answer the questions. If you are not unique, and the client has a choice between two or more restaurants that are the same, then it just comes down to pricing. And to get things straight, you cannot compete on price. There will always be that newbie restaurant that figures they can win the customer war by pricing. In the end, it hurts the restaurant and everyone involved with this strategy.

Classic examples can be taken from some of the big companies. Remember, they started off small, came up with a WMYU, and now are multibillion-dollar companies. Some examples include: "Pizza hot and fresh in 30 minutes or less." "When you absolutely have to have it there overnight," "We are number two but do our best." Some of my respected restaurants' WMYUs include: "All our ingredients are local sourced to offer the freshest, exciting meal possible," "We offer street food offerings that are on the wild side," "Your dining experience is in an environment conducive to lively chats and social drinking."

Once you create your own WMYU, then that message needs to be carried through in all your marketing strategies. There can be no conflict with the message. For example, if you say you offer a nice, quiet dining experience for romantic dates, then the guest should not experience a brightly lit environment with a live, loud band.

This is a hard exercise for sure. But there is some comfort in knowing that you can change your WMYU at any time. However, it is easy to declare. A little harder to change once you start getting the message out to your clients.

Towelettes – Mini Marketing

Do you have food items on your menu that entail using hands? If so, then printed mini towelettes (see resource chapter) might be an offering consideration. There is an enchanted aspect. The enchanted aspect is to do whatever you can that is unexpected and even over the top. You want to surprise the client. When the enchanted component comes into play, word of mouth and social media kick in to promote your restaurant.

There are some food niches in which moist packaged towelettes are expected. This includes those that offer hot wings, seafood, and sandwiches. But there are a surprising number of restaurants in these categories that do not offer towelettes.

Most clients, when offered towelettes, will either use them on the spot or stash them inside a purse or pocket. We just seem to not be able to let it go. We value the gesture and the convenience towelettes offer at that moment or in the future.

There are benefits to offering towelettes. The towelettes can become a mini business card and coupon. Think of them as mini billboards. With current technology, you can have the package printed on both sides with full color. Ideas for each side can be contact information, a promotion, links to landing pages, or a map. Another benefit is that the packaging process allows a shelf life of up to two years. Most business cards don't have a lifespan that compares.

Another option is to use one side of the packet for your restaurant and then offer advertising space for the other side. I currently work with an optometrist. His side of the packet has an eye test regarding reading the small letters that are printed on the packet.

Branding is not a primary purpose of getting clients into your restaurants. It takes a lot of money. It is hard to track. But in this case, branding gets boosted because you are enchanting the clients with your gesture of caring.

Target Market

Who is your ideal customer? That is the question, along with the WMYU question posed in another chapter. You need to determine this answer before any marketing commences. You need to have a visual in your mind of who your ideal client is regarding traits, hobbies, lifestyle, likes, dislikes, passions, etc. The more variables you can answer, the more powerful your reach to these clients is.

In the beginning, it may be a challenge to determine your target market. To get things started, it may be best to declare a zone of influence. This zone can be a five-mile radius around your restaurant. This is an adequate start.

You will find that a target market of a five-mile radius will work with your marketing efforts. But through time and variable analysis and testing, you will start to get an idea of the clients that frequent your restaurant.

It is important that you refer to this question constantly until you do have all the variables answered. Some of the places to look within your own marketing are the years born in your birthday marketing. Look at the zip codes in your information sheets. You can even look deeper into the street addresses. Look at the ticket sales for customers who take delivery. There is data everywhere.

If you start with the five-mile radius around your restaurant, you can get the demographic information of the households. A good place to get this information is the local Chamber of Commerce. The Chamber of Commerce usually has a packet of the demographics for the city. Information such as household income, housing prices, school and college graduates, types of jobs, and age groups. This is a great start.

Over time, you should have built a database of your clients. Of all the marketing tools and tips found in this book, the database is paramount. So if you are considering. Don't. Just do it. As stated, once you have built your database with a chunk of names, you can investigate further with your ideal client.

A technology tool to garner information is to use online surveys. Email to your client base to answer some simple questions. Mention that you value your clients and always trying to improve on experience, service, and quality. Most will oblige and complete the survey.

Standard questions such as zip code, income levels, age, and occupation segments can be asked. The question I like to ask is what type of magazine(s) they subscribe to. With that information, you will be able to refer to the magazine's demographic profile to gain even more insight about your client. These profiles convey to potential advertisers of the magazine the details of the typical reader. These magazines spend a lot of money to conduct surveys themselves. The good news is that this information is free. You just need to request from the publisher.

A side note is that more and more people are turning to digital content. So another question to add to your survey is that if they don't subscribe to a magazine, what magazine would they read if given a chance to subscribe. Often, this question can be answered.

Also, keep track of this response because when you get a super client, you want to reward him or her every so often. This can be in the form of a thank you note. However, a magazine subscription makes a great gift. Subscriptions today are very affordable but make a great impression on the client. Another tip is, at the end of the year, publishers have a gift program. If you subscribe to the magazine (can place into your restaurant), you can gift a year to someone for free. That would be your top clients.

If the online surveys do not get much of a response, then the next step is to actually snail mail the survey with a self-addressed stamped envelope. Explain the importance of the survey and ask that they complete it. And explain that in doing so, there will be a special gift for taking the time to complete. When the survey is returned, a gift card or coupon can be returned as a reward for completion.

If you neglect this and the WMYU, marketing will be an uphill battle and funds budgeted to marketing will not be as effective as they could be. And most dreaded, I don't want to you give up declaring marketing doesn't work. It does. Really. Trust me.

Marketing Calendar

In another chapter, there was a description of having a large pushpin board and dry erase board. With this chapter, another recommendation for your office wall is a large calendar. This calendar ships as one roll. It is designed with the months side by side starting with January on the very left side and December on the very right.

Calendars that are printed in flip chart or other display options really won't work well, although you are invited to research different formats that align with your planning techniques. This calendar is meant to be written on, posted on, and basically makes a great reference to plan and execute.

Some important things to add onto the calendar start with holidays and special days. You can find online special days. Typical days are Valentine's Day and Mother's Day. But there is so much more. Chances are that these obscure, popular days coincide and relate to your food service niche.

For example, there is National Tea Month, National Soup Month, Chocolate Cake Day, Thank a Mailman Day, and so much more. Can you already feel the creative wheels turning? You can literally take any of these days and months and implement an incredible campaign.

By the way, there is literally a special occasion for every day of the year. The reason is that it is so easy to create a special day. You just declare it. The hard part is actually getting people to recognize the day you created. But you can implement the traditional marketing you already learned, and maybe through the years, you will become famous for declaring this special day.

This created day can also be newsy enough to contact the media. You can create a press release (see chapter) and then send it out to the contact list you created for such an occasion. When published, you can also be viewed as authority in your industry. This doesn't hurt with your authority position in your segment at all.

As a side note, we often hear about special days or months with the word "national." Turns out that you really cannot declare a special day with this word. To be official, national days need to be declared by the President or Congress.

Obviously, you can probably get away with the word national. It lends importance and credibility. But with social media and all the communicative technology available, you will most likely get caught and garner more negative publicity than positive.

Another component you might want to include on your calendar is an assortment of color markers and color post-it notes. Having color-coded marking on you calendar is easier on the eyes, and you can hone in on a particular variable that you color coded.

Marketing Calendar

Another tool that is recommended for your wall calendar is a timeline. That is basically a horizontal line that starts on the day of implementation. Then the line is drawn horizontally through the months if needed and ends on the day that terminates the campaign. This is a great visual that will give you the goal and the start point. If you view this on a regular basis, you can't help to be affected by the urgency to complete.

Video

Video sites are an often-overlooked marketing weapon. It doesn't take sophisticated equipment, and lots of times, the content you are creating for your newsletter, website, and other media can be directly converted to video. Just mark in your calendar a shoot schedule and start filming. If there is a carrot on the stick, videos help with authority marketing. If the owner is being filmed, then there is a gravitation of the public perception upholding you as someone who is an authority in what you do. There comes respect and inclination to do business with you.

Another benefit of videos is they tend to get higher rankings in the search engines. Also, at the time of this writing, the search engines are showing a mini pic of a frame from the video. This helps with catching the eye of the searcher and hopefully following the link to your video.

Social Media

There are several social media applications to focus your attention on. Check the resource site or back of the book for up-to-date information. Unfortunately, I cannot devote much space to do marketing on these sites justice. It would take a book or several books to adequately cover in detail. But there is a big takeaway. Once you sign up on each of these sites, there is one thing you can do to make them effective for your restaurant. And that is to be active in adding and updating content. Daily is preferred. But we are running a restaurant and focusing on operations. I get it. But you gotta do what you gotta do.

Internet Necessities

The interspace or the internet is really an important marketing media. However, it has been used maybe too extensively by the world. It is not a bad thing. But all I'm suggesting is that you shouldn't abandon the other marketing mediums found in this book. It is easy to be convinced that the internet will solve everything.

But you do need to be involved with the major areas of the internet. As soon as possible, sign up and get your restaurant listed on several category sites. These sites include mapping sites, search engines, review sites, and travel recommendation sites. Unfortunately, it would take many chapters to list the step-by-step process to get listed for each site. But each site does have a FAQ or link to instructions to get listed.

If you are just getting started having your restaurant dive into the interspace, it is easy to get lost as to how and where to focus your attention. As of this writing, the following sites should be your first focus. But in the end, when time permits, you need to get listed or involved in all of the entities available. The question is how long is the list. A good start is to type in your style of niche and the city in a search engine. Note what restaurants get listed.

Then take the top restaurants listed and type them into the search engine. Note all of the sites that this restaurant is listed with.

The first site you get your restaurant listed with is with Google. This is still the largest and most popular search engine. Google is getting more popular in regards to a resource for customers to find restaurants. When you type in a style of food, a map is displayed with various restaurants that cater to the niche. If your restaurant is not listed, you need to make it a priority to get listed. Unfortunately, this takes a little time. Google requires a verification process that can take up to several weeks to process.

Once registered with Google, you need to update as much information about your restaurant, including professional pictures. When you follow the link to the map, a side box is displayed with everything about the business a customer would like to know, including hours, pictures, menu, and reviews.

An equally important site to register your restaurant with is Yelp. This is a search engine rating site. If your restaurant has been in business for a while, chances are that it's already listed on Yelp. You need to register the listing so that you can access the dashboard. The dashboard contains information that basically describes your customer base without the name. This is important information when creating marketing campaigns to cater to a demographic.

You should check both Google and Yelp on a regular basis. Reviews are important in two aspects. The first aspect is that if there are bad reviews, you can see if there are any issues with food, quality, and service. If this is an absentee ownership situation, this is even more important. When the owner is away . . . anyways, reviews will describe the issues and can be addressed with the team members.

The second aspect is reviews must be answered and replied to. This includes good and bad reviews. The faster the better. It seems that clients dare the restaurants to answer to their reviews and check back on their own reviews to see what the owner is going to do. Clients still call on the phone if they encountered a not-so-good experience, but more and more, it seems that the reviews is the place clients go to express their issues.

Therefore, reviews need to be addressed. Other people will obviously read the review and the reply. Everyone would like to see how it's resolved or replied to. The good news is that your competitors are probably not replying to their reviews. Your business will look like the business that cares.

And there is something else you can do to give yourself a perspective on the popularity of your restaurant. Verbally ask your mobile phone app, tablet, computer, or home assistant. Ask "where is the best (Insert category) restaurant near me." You might be surprised at the answer. If it is not your restaurant, that might be your goal to get it as a reply from the assistant.

Domain Name

Creating a website is mandatory. People can argue that social media and search engines replace the website, thus making it obsolete. But if there is an argument for a website, it would be that it is still found in the search engines. If you get ranked on the first page, you have a good chance of being noticed.

As stated before, ranking through SEO (Search Engine Optimization) is really challenging and consumes a chunk of a restaurant owner's time. In other words, there is no time to dedicate all resources to be ranked.

However, there is good news. A local restaurant has a good chance of being ranked high for several reasons. The first is that a local search yields companies in that particular area. If a restaurant is searched via city, it has a very good chance of being ranked high because you will come to find that your competitors don't have a website. Or the website is so poorly executed that the web crawlers (algorithms that go through a website to read and rank) conclude the website is not substantial enough to rank or unreadable. The web crawlers may deem it not important.

Domain Name

An aspect of a website is the domain name. A domain name is the address to your website. A customer types in the domain name into a browser and then is led to the website.

It is important that you register your own name for several reasons. Having a registered name lends credibility to your site. There are free domain names, but the address is long or obfuscated because it is part of the primary company's domain. It's a sub-domain. With your own domain, you can make it short and memorable.

Domain names are also low priced. For under $20, you can own a domain for a year. It's like buying real estate. You are purchasing a place in the interspace. It is your location. This is such a huge concept because with that price, you can purchase multiple domain names. The reason why is you can point the multiple domains to the same site.

Imagine you are searching the internet for a place to eat. You would probably type in the style of food and city. Another popular search is the style of food with the words "nearby." The reason why you want to type city is because you are not interested in a restaurant listed in the search engine from another country or far away.

To help with the search ranking, you want to pick several domain names. The first domain name is with the words of your restaurant. This is more to protect the name. If someone were to register your restaurant name as a domain name, they could use the name for monetary gain. This is more likely to happen when your restaurant becomes popular and famous. A person can then create a website with the domain name of your restaurant to drive traffic there. If you want to flip this strategy, you can purchase domain names of your competitor.

Or they could increase the selling price of the domain name knowing that you will need to purchase to control. It is possible to take the other company to court, but litigation is a headache and a mess.

After you register your restaurant name, the next domain name is the generic term domain name. For example, you want to register the domain name using the type of niche and city. Then type the type of niche with the word "nearby."

In other words, you want to lock up multiple domain names that can mirror the user typing in the search engine. Although algorithms change with the search engine, having the keywords in your domain name does help with the rankings.

In the future, there is a good chance that you will cash out of the business. Part of the assets to value include fixtures. But you can definitely put a value on digital assets such as domain names, websites, and databases. You always need to forward think.

Digital Signs

Digital signs are as the name suggests. Utilizing new generation flat screens that are high in resolution, clients cannot help but look. Signs are important in restaurants. They lend to the décor of the restaurant, convey specials, and highlight menu items. With marketing, signage reminds or informs clients of birthday cards, gift certificates, and rewards programs. In the old days, if one wanted to change or update signage, it entailed going to the printer, whether from a desktop or a professional.

Gone are the days of time wasted taking down, printing, and then hanging up new signs. With digital signs, messages can be changed instantly. This saves money on printing. Digital signs can be animated to bring messages to life. Live feeds, such as news, weather, and travel, can be displayed.

I think one of the best aspects of digital signs is that they can be programmed wirelessly. Digital signs can run on Wi-Fi, which means no wires. Digital messages can be developed from a computer on location or from home. Everything is done through the internet.

Digital Signs

Other uses for digital signs are to display full menus. Prices and pictures can be changed quickly. The menus can be displayed at different times of the day. For example, if you have lunch specials, the digital signs can display the lunch menu prominently and then disappear for the dinner slot.

Chalkboards are still popular and do lend themselves to the décor. But digital signs can even emulate a chalkboard through a chalkboard background and chalk font.

You can create your own presentations via a computer. A PowerPoint presentation can be set up and set to play on a loop. However, the presentation is just enough to scrape by. A better way is to subscribe to a service that actually is set up for digital signage.

For example, a nominal fee will allow you to access the specialized site. Here, you will be able to stitch together a program that will rival any of the big chains' digital signage. Apps are available on these sites that are even more specialized. There are apps just for weather, news, notices, and menus. They make it easy for a technology novice to drag and drop, cut and paste, and type and create.

There are many services that offer this type of business model. You can find the latest update at the resource section.

The other option is to move the next level up and subscribe to a service that actually creates the media and drives the content to your flat screens. But the tradeoff is that it is more expensive. You're trading your time to pay for someone else's. The decision is yours.

Digital Signs

Remember that you still need to think like a direct marketer. Every dollar spent must return that same dollar or more. If you are paying $1 or $100 for the digital sign, you need to track and analyze. This can get kind of tricky because it is tempting to splash up on the flat screen a menu item. But the question is if the client orders the item because he or she already ordered from the past or found it in the printed menu.

You can place a special code on the flat screen and have the client mention the code. But I've found that the team members are already strapped for time and always seem to be multi-tasking. They are hesitant to go through extra steps just to get the order through. They don't see the importance of registering a code.

What works, as of late, is to actually have a promotion or menu item that cannot be found elsewhere except for the digital sign. Then when ordered, you will be able to conclude it was ordered through the digital sign.

Remember what you learned from past chapters. Every slide that finds its way to the digital sign needs a headline, benefits, testimonials, a call to action, and a deadline. And the big takeaway is to always test. This is very easy in this case because everything is digital. You don't need to print different tests. It can be changed instantly and programmed to show whatever time of day you wish.

Autoresponders

The goal of the client relationship is to keep in constant contact with the client. This is especially important when someone signs up for any of your various programs such as birthdays, rewards, and newsletters (details found in other chapters).

On the surface, this seems like an arduous task. A customer signs up for a program. Then you send a welcome and thank you email. Then in a couple of days, you send another email. A couple of days later, another email is sent.

Soon, there is a realization that this is a very time-consuming task. And the other aspect is keeping track of the emails sent. However, there is good news regarding this once time-consuming task.

A special email category exists called autoresponders. This title suggests what these emailers do. When a customer signs up for your program, an automatic email is sent out. Then, determined by you, subsequent emails are sent for as long as the messages and the timeframes are set.

This is an incredible timesaver. While these emails are sent in the background, you can expend more energy in driving traffic to your client funnel. You can even incorporate past newsletters in the autoresponder. A whole year can be loaded into the system. And each month (or similar), the newsletter is sent. On the client side, they think that you created the newsletter at the moment.

There are several leading companies that offer autoresponders. Because technology and recommendations change, the current listing can be found on the website via the resource page at the end of the book. Companies may change. But the technology, function, and place in marketing stays the same.

Bartering – nugget

Bartering offers a unique way to garner services and products at a reduced rate. There are organizations found in areas that specialize in connecting businesses through a barter exchange.

At the simple level, a business purchases a widget at a wholesale price (standard process) and then sells at retail. If you purchased the item for $50 and sold at $100, you make a profit of $50. With bartering, you still sell your item for $100, and instead of receiving American currency, there is a credit or barter bucks.

You can then take these barter bucks and purchase goods and services. If the goods and services are $100, then you just received the goods and services at half price because you originally paid $50 in the beginning of the process.

Running a restaurant entails services throughout the year. For me, plumbing and HVAC is at the top of the list. I purposely seek small businesses in which the owner is the person that comes to service.

Autoresponders

It has become a habit in which I ask if the owner would like to barter food for service. If the service was billed at $100, I trade the service for gift certificates or gift cards that total up to the service. Sometimes, the owner will trade one to one. However, there are instances in which they garner equipment or employee costs for the service and cannot trade at full cost. But the majority of the time, a barter deal can be established in which both parties benefit.

Here's how the numbers crunch. Food costs are around 30 percent. Without accounting for the other costs related to overhead and operations, a hundred-dollar service call essentially cost $30. Yes, that is not the true cost, but I think that one realizes that there was not a cash outlay, and there was an overall savings on the transaction.

Another opportunity for bartering is through advertising publications. There are local shopper mailers found throughout the country. I work with a publication (see resource chapter) that prints a half page color advertisement and mails throughout the county. There is a barter agreement in which there is no cash outlay.

The publisher has an arrangement in which they are allowed to sell twenty gift certificates to the public that are redeemable at the restaurant. To entice sales, the gift certificates have a face value of $30. However, the publisher sells the gift certificate at half face value of $15.

The bottom line is that the certificate purchaser may redeem at the restaurant for the face value of $30. The restaurant's cost is 30 percent. The gift certificates have a deadline in which the $30 value reverts back to the original cost of $15 if not redeemed in a timely manner.

If you find a publisher that is willing and able to work with this business model, make sure that you do not fall into the trap of having their art department create the ad. Remember the information found throughout the book. You still need to adhere to all the traditional marketing that has proven to work for centuries.

Remember that the essential elements are required such as headlines. An eye-catching picture helps. List the benefits. Make sure to include an offer with a deadline. You also want to add testimonials. Add the various ways of finding you, such as social media addresses and website addresses.

To ensure that your business is not affected by redemptions ten years in the future, you may create your own special certificates with a deadline. This will help keep your margins in check because restaurants are affected by so many variables that seem to increase every year.

As you know, the short of the long includes food costs, utilities, rent, operations, and seasonal COGS that just seem to keep rising. The caveat is that your state or jurisdiction may have restrictions. It is advisable to check with your network of advisors, such as accountant and lawyer.

Big Extreme Contest

Can you think of offering one of your dishes as an extreme contest offer? Some people in the industry might call this gimmicky. But there are aspects of this marketing that are still valid and still might be worth considering. Again, the underlying recommendation is to test.

To elaborate on the extreme contest offer, the best way is to give examples. A Vietnamese restaurant offers the Pho bowl challenge. The owner purchased a special bowl that was five times as large as the standard bowl. Any guest that accepts the challenge needs to consume everything, including the broth. If this feat can be accomplished within thirty-five minutes, then the soup is comped. Otherwise, the guest pays the listed price.

In another restaurant, if the challenge is accepted, an omelet is created using twelve eggs. Within the omelet are also fillings such as bacon, potato, and veggies. You need to consume this in its entirety within the hour by yourself. Any guest that can accomplish this gets a free t-shirt and the meal is also comped. The other reward is recognition. The picture of the super guest is taken and posted on the restaurant's wall of fame.

Big Extreme Contest

The newsy aspect of this marketing promotion is still relevant. Can you imagine all the selfies, postings, and likes a guest will get from social media exposure? And your restaurant name is printed all over the dishes and eating ware. If the contestant wins, then they showcase their bulging stomach in their new t-shirt—again for social media.

The commonality with these other restaurants is that even though these are common dishes, they coined special names for the contest. You can and should do the same. That way, you have a dish that is unique for your restaurant. In the future, you can offer the smaller portion of the contest dish with the same name. You can designate the dish with "Jr." or "human portion," etc.

Getting to the wall of fame. You do need this also because people like to re-visit with their friends and families and brag about the time when they won the food challenge. Their friends will then say that they already know because they saw it all over social media, in which case the reply is that they are showing proof that it happened.

Business Cards
Double sided, QR code, goes to landing page.

Business cards have always been perceived as a necessary tool for contact information. That still holds true. However, business cards can be so much more. For example, being that this is prime real estate, any blank areas are a lost opportunity. This is especially true of the back. I collect business cards and a good majority of cards are blank on the back. I have been known to use the backs to jot notes whenever the occasion arises.

Don't let your business card turn into a bookmark, become a note, or end up in the round file. Basically, the business card needs to have a reason to be kept. The business card should have all the pertinent information, such as a phone number, website address, name of restaurant, hours, etc.

However, the business card should be a means to act. The card can have a special domain name that when a visitor accesses it, you know it came from the business card. A good promotion is to get a free gift card by going to the website. The domain address takes the visitor to a landing page where they complete a form to receive the gift card.

Business Cards

Make it a mini sales letter with a headline. The headline can be at the very edge at the top so that if placed in a wallet, it can be read among the other cards. Bullet points should be a part of the components. Then a testimonial or two would help to make this a sales piece versus a standard business card.

Another promotion is a type of reward card. On the card, there are a number of pics, dots, and numerals printed in rows and columns. Each time the client visits the restaurant, the card is initialed over the printing to indicate a visit or purchase. Once all the visits are complete, then the client receives a new card and a gift. The gift should be substantial, such as an entrée or dessert or similar.

Remember that a good promotion is asking the client to act. But also give a reason why they need to act in a timely manner. A deadline or expiration is a good component to add into the verbiage of the promotion.

Another component that can be added into the business card is a QR code. A QR code is a specially designed icon that when scanned by a mobile phone, takes the client to a website via phone. This convenience bypasses the step of typing in your website address.

Generating unique QR codes are free and easy. Look at the resources at the end of the book for links. Or just search QR code generator on any search engine.

Clean Bathrooms

Log sign, graffiti, smell, air dryer (pros/cons), adverts, IPad surveys

Why is a chapter titled bathrooms in a restaurant success book? Did you know by repetitive surveys and comments that bathrooms are the top mentions through verbal and written comments?

Through time, I have considered bathrooms to be an integral part of marketing. In fact, if you don't take this seriously, any marketing that you have established and implemented can be negated in an instant.

Hopefully, I have scared you enough to read this chapter in all seriousness. You see, clean bathrooms are probably one of the most important variables and considerations for restaurant success.

And to reflect, think of a time when you visited a restaurant for the first time. Was the bathroom clean? If not, what were your thoughts? There were times when I visited the bathroom before ordering. My perception of the food, the kitchen, and the prep was pretty much determined by the bathroom visit. It has become habit for me to visit the bathroom of every restaurant and eatery whenever I dine out.

You need to make bathrooms an important focus when your restaurant is open. The bathroom needs to be cleaned and stocked more than one time per day. There are times between cleaning when trash ends up on the floor or dispensers run dry. That can't be avoided. But you can imply that the restrooms are on vigil.

You want to have a bathroom cleaning log on display in the bathroom. This log is in full view of the client. When they see it, they are assured that you care for the cleanliness and safety of the customer. And if there is trash or dispensers run dry, the client can extrapolate that you do attend to the matters but maybe this is just a fluke. Also, on the log or sign is a statement on how much you care, and if the level of standards is not to your liking, please contact management immediately.

The log also holds team members accountable. If they don't sign the log, then you know that the restroom was not cleaned. And if they fake the signing and a client complains, you can address the comment to the team member. They will need to explain why the restroom was in that state of condition.

Another sign you want to place in view of everyone is that the employees must wash their hands. This again sends a comforting message to the client that your company cares about health and safety. And again, this helps to remind team members of the expectations of the restaurant.

Think of the restroom as an independent entity. What would you need to do to make customers of the bathroom happy? What can you do to make the environment inviting? One of the popular components is to add music. Music has its positives. It adds mood and feeling. But it also hides extra noises if you know what I mean.

Flowers or fake flowers are a nice touch. Pictures are awesome because it can extend the tone of the interior of the dining room. It can also make a statement about the focus of making this interior and independent entity. There is an Italian restaurant chain that has pictures of people urinating (it is done in good taste). The pictures lend humor and serves as a distraction for people waiting to use the facilities. It's a busy restaurant.

Hand dryers also need to be considered. There has been a study that hand blow dryers actually blow around bacteria and smells. And they are loud. Tough call because paper has its own negatives, which include environmental waste.

On the topic of graffiti. It's going to happen at some point if it hasn't already. The most important step is to clean or remove it before the next business day. Graffiti is a cancer and will grow if even left unaddressed for a couple of days. If you are an absentee owner establishment, you need to send the important message to the team members that graffiti must be reported to you so that you can act.

You need to have protocols to address graffiti. Extra paint for the walls needs to be stored conveniently. The walls can be painted after closing. Don't wait. With porcelain, there is special porcelain paint available, and you want to keep some on hand. Mirrors need to be replaced.

Clean Bathrooms

Metal is a tough material. With chromed piping, instead of replacing, I have actually taken a knife and made random scratches to make the graffiti unreadable. With metal stalls, I have a cordless grinder with a low abrasive to "polish" the walls.

Wood is easier to work with. Crayons to fill scratches, sandpaper to scuff, stain and paint to finish. Basically, most materials can be repaired to delay replacing. Again, the takeaway is that graffiti must be removed within twenty-four hours.

Smells are obviously one of the major issues. Sometimes you get a guest that is over productive. That just goes with the territory. Depending on the layout of the bathroom and access, there are air fresheners available. Tough solution in this case because this is a variable with many answers.

Even with bathrooms, you can enchant the client. Have you ever considered after washing your hands and you exiting that maybe the door handle has bacteria infestations from those that don't wash their hands? Some clients actually have a habit to counter this question by opening the handle with another paper towel. The problem is that the waste paper basket is near the sink, farther away from the door.

Then the option is to try to be a basketball player and throw the wad at the basket. Near misses and misses end up on the floor. Does anyone take the time to pick up the paper, wash their hands again, open the door with a paper towel, and then throw again? Probably not.

Clean Bathrooms

Therefore, you want to enchant your clients by having a basket near the door. And there is actually a product that is a dispenser with a smaller sized paper to open the door.

Lastly, there are products available that can be mounted on a wall or stand that looks like a tablet. But its only function is to ask the client a couple of questions about the bathroom. It asks for cleanliness, experience, dispensers, etc. Besides some useful information for you, this survey device gives the impression to the client how important restrooms are to your establishment.

Co-Op Advertising / Co-Op With Other Tenants

Co-op advertising is not really a marketing campaign tactic or strategy. But the use of co-op advertising can definitely make your marketing spending go further. Thus, you are able to test and implement more.

Co-op advertising is when a vendor, distributor, or anyone you have a relationship with that keeps your restaurant running. This is usually in the form of other business entities helping to pay for your advertisements. There is a tradeoff that needs to benefit them.

This tradeoff is their product or service needs to be recognized in some way. In my case, I was importing a beer that was new to the country. The representative was trying his hardest to gain a foothold in the market. At the time, I needed new menus printed. We agreed that if I put pics in the menu of his product, he would pay for half the cost of the menus.

I also worked with my soda representative to print banners and signage. The caveat is that posters and banners can become a logo fest with their products printed everywhere. But the representative worked with me to create a banner with minimal product logos and wording. It matched the décor and tone of the restaurant.

Have you ever priced a sandwich sign? These are the signs found outdoors in front of the restaurant that are hinged at the top. Anyways, they are expensive. But my representative was able to send me one for free.

If you work with one of the two big cola companies, you will find a wealth of materials that are there for the taking. You will have a local representative with an authorized budget to spend with your restaurant. If you don't use it, another restaurant will.

There is another co-op opportunity. You can work with your neighbors and pool together to get a full-page ad in the local magazine. These advertisements are costly. But if you and your neighbors each take a piece of the display ad, you can all benefit from garnering more attention because of the size of the advertisement.

Digital Billboard

Billboards in the past were a tough channel. Static printed billboards were expensive, and testing was also a challenge because often a business was locked in for a period from a month and beyond. But technology has changed this medium.

There are now digital billboards. They are rotating, which means multiple ads are changed on a regular basis. There is good and bad with the rotations. The good is that this model has brought the cost down dramatically. Your ad is shown for a fraction of a minute (ten seconds) and shown throughout the day. For around $20 a day, the ad might show hundreds of times. Of course, this depends on location and times of day (peak and off peak).

The other benefit is that getting content on the board is instant. You simply upload your content and schedule. The board starts working immediately by displaying your advertisement. The ad spending is also capped. You set the limit and will not be charged past your limit.

And yet another benefit is that you can test. You can upload an ad, and you will know when it displays. The message needs to call for an action and have an urgency, such as limited supplies and deadline. You can split test. You compare one ad to another. You can test time of day. You can test location. You can test messages. You can test messages for the time of day. For example, if it is lunchtime, you can advertise lunch specials.

The bad is that your ad is shown for a fraction of the time a normal billboard displays. Traffic and viewers that would normally see a static billboard will miss your message at any given moment.

The bad is that this is a new business model and there are not that many self-serve digital boards. The big cities and urban areas seem to have this technology. But the rural areas are much less so. But in the future, and probably soon, this technology will be prevalent.

80/20 Rule

A lot has been thrown at you in this book. And if you were to do everything listed yourself, you won't have time to sleep. There is the likelihood of getting burned out or just not implementing anything.

There is a time hack that I would like to share. The recommended process is to implement as many programs as possible. Through analytics, you will be able to determine what is working. It is a goal to have your marketing funnel being filled by various sources of campaigns that bring in new clients. Whenever one campaign becomes ineffective, the others will keep providing.

However, the other side of the coin is to choose a handful of effective campaigns and excel at implementing them. Realize that I'm still advocating multiple streams of clients into your funnel. It's just a matter of paring down these campaigns verses having numerous campaigns that cannot be tended by you. There needs to be a focus.

To guide you with your focus, there is a rule called the 80/20 rule. This rule was recognized by a detailed observer named Vilfredo Pareto. This rule is also known as the Pareto Principle.

Essentially, the rule states that 80 percent of an effect is from 20 percent of the source or input. An example that he noted was that 80 percent of the wealth in Italy was attributed to 20 percent of the people. Another example is that 80 percent of the land is controlled by 20 percent of the people. Twenty percent of your wardrobe is worn 80 percent of the time.

This rule can be applied to everything with a very small variability. I challenge you to open your senses and try to attribute everything to the Pareto Principle. In the restaurant, if the rule holds true, 80 percent of your sales is from 20 percent of the menu items. Eighty percent of your sales are from 20 percent of your clients.

As you drill down the analysis and observation, the Pareto Principle still works. For example, with the menu items, 80 percent of the menu sales are from 20 percent of the items. If you take the menu items and apply the principle again, you will find that 80 percent of the sales of those menu items are from 20 percent of the items. You can keep doing this until there are no menu items left. Another example with restaurants is that 80 percent of the tips are derived from 20 percent of the servers. I can't resist. I'm sorry, here's another. Eighty percent of complaints are from 20 percent of clients. Okay, I'll stop.

With marketing, you will see that 80 percent of the effectiveness will be derived from 20 percent of your marketing campaigns. Once you are able to determine the 20 percent of the campaigns, you can eliminate the other campaigns.

You can then drill down within that campaign. For example, if you determine that out of all your campaigns, you find that sending direct mailouts is the most effective in returning your dollars spent, then you can apply the 80/20 rule again within this campaign. You may find that letters with a particular headline are getting 80 percent of the effective results. Then you can keep drilling down all the variables until there are none left.

Another important focus with the 80/20 rule is your clients. You will find that 20 percent of your clients are directly responsible for 80 percent of your sales. You can then drill down within your database and find that within the 20 percent of your clients, 20 percent again is responsible for 80 percent of that chunk. If the principle holds true, you will find that only a handful of clients are responsible for a big part of your sales.

With that said, you will want to ensure that this handful of clients is well taken care of and recognized as a part of your success. You will want to send extra special correspondences and gratitude.

Another focus is toward your team members. You will find that 20 percent of your team members are the cause of 80 percent of your challenges faced by your restaurant. This could be in the form of bad reviews, bad quality in food prep and service, and operations. Once determined who they are, you will want to remedy the situation accordingly.

Then the next step is once you have the 20 percent campaigns, you will further observe that among those campaigns, 20 percent is carrying 80 percent of effectiveness. An example is that you have ten campaigns that are acquiring new clients. You will find that two of the campaigns are bringing 80 percent of the new customers.

The huge implication is that every unit of time that you expend will be more effective and waste is reduced. Go ahead and try it in your life and your business.

Facebook Check In

Technology can seem gimmicky at times. We can never know how long a tactic or strategy can last. But for now, Facebook check-ins are worth the time to implement. With Facebook check-ins, a client arrives at your restaurant to dine. When he or she settles in, they probably will be using their mobile phones.

Facebook is usually one of the stops as they rotate between apps, texting, and emails. But when a client gets to Facebook, some will actuate a function called "Check-in." Think of it as them telling their friends and family that they are checking in to let everyone know where they are at.

Now forward think to how this could help your restaurant. If a diner has two hundred followers on Facebook and they check-in at your restaurant, they just notified everyone that they are dining at your restaurant. Then the bad guys break into their homes and rob them. Just kidding.

But no, really, when they are checking in, a map shows up with your location and the name of the restaurant. If you scale this process up to multiple guests at any given time, your restaurant is forever etched on everyone's thread. People will see the check-in, and even later, they will be scrolling through the pages and see the check-in again.

It's just multiple exposure of your restaurant without actually paying for advertising. It's even an endorsement by someone they know. And it is even like word-of-mouth marketing.

A way to get guests to check-in is to ask. You can verbally ask to check-in or have signs posted. A promotion to prod guests is that if they check-in and show their mobile phone during their stay, they will get something in return. The standard comp is free dessert or appetizer.

The challenging aspect is tracking results. You can track how many people check-in inside your restaurant. But it is challenging to know how many people actually come into your restaurant because of the original check-in. If you are using the above promotion, you are giving away food for a question mark. That is why, now, it is worth implementing but really shouldn't be at the top of the marketing list.

Family Meal Deals

If you want to increase the average ticket price, then this might be a promotion that you might consider. And there is good news. You can get your drink vendor to help with the cost.

Guests have time constraints. They want convenience. They want value. This is called the family meal deal. For a price, a set package is offered. This package can vary. Think about how you can put together a meal for an average family. This case is for two adults and two youths.

Then make a meal with an entrée and a side or two. Then price it at retail. To make the deal more special, you need to add a freebie. Options include another side, appetizer, or soft drinks.

This promotion works well. In fact, a year ago, I noticed a similar promotion on a busy freeway billboard. It is a static display. The deal is a family meal deal of five hamburgers, five fries, and five soft drinks for $15.99. I know that this deal works because the advertisement on the billboard has not changed for over a year. If it didn't work, the advertisement would have been changed or scratched altogether.

Family Meal Deals

Observing advertisements that don't change or are repeated for an extended time is a great way to get ideas to emulate. You can be assured that the add is pulling unless they are on a branding spending spree. But you already know how to spot a direct response type of advertisement. Build your swipe files, and thus, your arsenal.

Getting to the other part of the promotion. If you decide to use the free drink option, you can work with your drink vendor representative. If you are using one of the big two companies, then it is very likely that they will have a promotion budget to help you out with the meal deal.

They can print the promotion for free. To benefit the drink company, somewhere on the printing has to include their logo, drink name, and a picture of the product. It doesn't need to dominate the space, but it does need to be on there somewhere.

I had the representative print me some window clings and table tents. I also made the promotion good for dine-in only. That way, if was I going to lose some margin, then the dining room needed to be occupied. This gives the perception of popularity. Nothing draws a crowd like a crowd.

The soft drink companies mentioned that this is a popular promotion. And even had templates available for the family meal deal at the print house. In fact, while we are on the topic, your representative and any vendor are great sources for promotion information.

When asked, they will tell you about promotions that are working for other restaurants. It's really easy to have blinders on and copy the competitor's promotions and advertising. The same niche restaurants are notorious for copying each other. Or you may have come to find out that your competitors don't even advertise at all. This is good news for you because you have an arsenal in your hands.

Read every chapter. Read every tactic and strategy. Then deploy and win.

Free Snack Before and After Meal

I like this tactic because it enchants the guests. They don't expect it the first time they come to the restaurant. And it uses a human element found in everyone. It's called reciprocity. It works. With reciprocity, a free sample is given away. You see this in malls, events, fairs, stores, everywhere.

Once the free sample is given away, the recipient feels obligated to re-balance the scales by purchasing. If the sample was food, the caveat is that the food has to taste good.

For your restaurant, you can use this human nature tool to enchant your guests. Think about something you can give away. Most eating establishments that use this method give away noodles with dipping sauce (Chinese restaurants), tortilla chips with dips (Mexican restaurants), and breadsticks (Italian restaurants).

Ideally, you want to give before they order in hopes that the order will be larger. But if not, maybe the reciprocity will happen for dessert. The question is what you can give for your restaurant. Can you give something unique? If your restaurant falls into one of the ethnic categories above, there might already be expectations from your guests. Minimally you can give away house sauce with the chips that is uniquely yours.

I myself found these products called shrimp chips. They come in little chunky disks that look like plastic. When deep fried, they expand into what looks like sponge chips. But they are crispy. They come in different colors. They enchant.

At the end of the meal, there is another opportunity for this. Restaurants give away mints, candy, fortune cookies, and hand wipes. The reciprocity aspect is to get larger tips. Or minimally, the goodwill is given before they leave the restaurant in hopes it lingers with them outside the doors. Enchant your guests, and you will be on social media, repeat visits, and word-of-mouth marketing. It's worth it.

Freelancers and Personal Assistants

There is this notion, from an owner's point of view, that he or she must do everything to get things done correctly. But as you can see, the tactics and strategies offered in this book would take a long time to implement.

There aren't enough hours in the day to set in place and then execute the marketing. If you haven't come to the realization now, I guarantee that you will. One of the paradigm shifts that hit me was the fact that I could not have a team member carry the load of my marketing. They were already time strapped as it was.

I couldn't hire a new team member because the marketing elements required didn't require a steady time slot for any one person. At that point, that was when I realized that my time was more important developing the marketing versus executing and collecting data.

That's when I found freelancers. I must admit that it is very hard to let go of some of the responsibilities to another individual. It's hard because you want to make sure that the job and task is done right and at a high level.

Freelancers and Personal Assistants

But my perception changed after a time. I realized that freelancers completed the project at probably a better level than what I could do. But most importantly, it freed up my time to work on implementing and creating more marketing projects and programs.

There are several freelancer sites. At the resource page of this book, you will find information on the sites that I recommend and use. Try it out. You will be delighted with the outcome and the time freed up.

This topic also transitions into the subject of personal assistants. Personal assistants are as the name suggests. Personal assistants can be considered as freelancers. Whereas freelancers are more for projects, a personal assistant is an ongoing task and project person.

A personal assistant does everything that you don't want to do. Here is the mindset. Marketing is probably the most important endeavor you will need to focus on to ensure the success of your restaurant. You may be able to push some of the tasks of marketing to freelancers and team members. However, you do need to oversee everything.

The next question is that if you are focused on the marketing aspect of your restaurant and it correlates to the success and income of your restaurant, then what is your time worth? Is it $10 per hour? Is it $50 per hour? Probably $100 to $1,000 per hour. Really hard to accept in the beginning. It was for me. But I promise that you will come to accept this premise one day. Hopefully soon. And when you do, your thinking about your time and importance to your business shifts into a whole different mode.

With that said, when you determine that your time is worth say $100 per hour, then any task that you are considering must be looked at and compared to your hourly wage. For example, if you need to take your clothes to the cleaners or change the oil in your car, is that task worth $100 per hour or can you pay someone $10 per hour to complete?

If so, you have just bought yourself a couple more hours in the day. Do you realize that if you can do this daily, then you gained fourteen more hours in the week or fifty-six hours in the month? That is incredible. You bought time.

Know this. You just gained more time in your life. Marketing should be the focus of gained time. But could you use that extra time to spend with your family? When those hours add up, could you use that surplus time to go on a vacation? Life is short.

Local Bloggers, Foodies, Reviewers

If you are confident with your food, service, and appearance of your restaurant, then a way to get recognition for your restaurant is to peruse the media. The goal is to reach out to writers, bloggers, and reviewers that could write about your food and restaurant.

The first place to look is to your local newspaper or television show that reviews restaurants. If they review your restaurant favorably, you can re-purpose the reviews in the form of hanging the review on the wall (print) or play the video of the review on the website, restaurant, or internet video sites.

A lot of print newspapers have digital versions online along with the writer and reviewer contact information. The same goes for cable and network shows. You can access their website and be able to find the contact information.

The next step is to reach out to social media and the internet. You are looking for foodies, writers, and bloggers with a big following. But you need to look for those that are local and will be able to come into your restaurant to eat, take pictures, and review.

In other words, you want that person to be able to dine in your restaurant.

There is going to be some time involved in researching. I like to go to each social media app and then search categories such as foodie, food reviews, and the city and local cities near your restaurant.

Lastly, you want to check Yelp for reviews of restaurants in your area. You want to focus your attention on the reviews from people who have a lot of reviews with other restaurants. The other signal is that they take a lot of pictures and their reviews are long and detailed. They also have many friends. Simply send a simple message telling the reviewer about your restaurant and invite them to try you out.

One last tip with Yelp is that if you decide to reach out to reviewers, read their reviews. Some reviewers are really critical and seem to only write about the negative side of the experience. There are many reviewers to choose from, and you can definitely find those that understand situations and are empathetic to the dining experience and will review fairly.

Local Sourcing and Support – Local Ingredients

Local sourcing and relationships have benefits. If you have a local farmer's market, you can start the communication about purchasing goods for your restaurant. Besides supporting the local businesses, you will also create the pathway toward word-of-mouth referrals. When a customer purchases from the vendor, the seller could recommend your restaurant as a place of use for their product.

Location does matter, and you might be in a location that does not have access to local growers and producers. But you can lengthen the supply chain and look further out. You might be surprised what you may find within your immediate area.

Products that are sourced include vegetables, eggs, fruits, honey, grains, and dairy. There are even some vendors that go a step further and process the raw materials. For example, citrus and fruit growers create their own juices. You can take advantage of this by offering and stating that the product is locally source and is unique for your establishment.

You can even private label the product and state that the recipe is unique to your restaurant. Then you can add that it was produced locally without any preservatives or artificial ingredients.

You can reciprocate by posting in your restaurant that you support local sources. You can then list the vendors and the raw materials that you use. These are also great newsworthy stories for your newsletter, blog posts, and social media. You want to spotlight a vendor and do a mini interview.

Subscribers like the slice of life and human interest stories. The subscribers also like to know how the product is grown or produced. Is it healthy? Is it organic? How are the livestock treated and fed? These are great questions to answer for all your channels of marketing.

Another benefit of local sourcing is that there is a perception of better quality and freshness. Clients feel that the short supply chain offers a better product that translates to a better prepared and tasting dish.

There is a story of two competing restaurants. They were literally across the street from each other. They both had similar food offerings. Both had similar establishment offerings such as dine-in, take-out, and delivery. However, one was more established and had a foothold in the market.

The newer restaurant owner was saddened by the fact that his business was losing money and seeing the other restaurant across the street packed with diners most of the time they were opened.

But one day, the newer restaurant owner came to the conclusion that if he could change the perception of the client, then he would win over the customer base and beat the competition.

It was an easy fix but an incredible insight on the owner. What he did was take the food that he was already using and display it in the dining room. This entailed all the vegetables and fruits. What he did was create a double-sided wall. One side was clear. Daily, he would fill the wall with the vegetables and fruit. During the day, the team members from the kitchen would take product as needed.

The perception to the clients was that the food being cooked in the kitchen was using fresh produce. If there was any thought of the restaurant using canned goods or processed vegetables, it was dispelled by seeing the actual product in the display wall.

It turns out that the competing restaurant also used fresh produce and fruits. It just came down to perception. Maybe the older established restaurant was originally perceived as being the better restaurant, but that changed with a little modification to the interior.

Mailing List 101

Compiled list, responder list, hotline list (recent buyers), repeat buyers.

Basically, a company or a list broker that provides a mailing list has names and addresses of people that would ideally be receptive to your offering. There is a hierarchy of renting mailing lists. And at each level of the hierarchy, the price and responsiveness changes accordingly.

The compiled list is at the lower level. Here, names and addresses are gathered according to some commonality. As it applies to restaurant marketing, a popular compiled list is homeowners. Another compiled list could be families with children. Another compiled list is names and addresses in a particular zip code.

The compiled list is cheaper per name and address. Maybe you can see why this list can be effective. But at times, this list can be considered general in nature. Therefore, the response rate is expectedly not very high.

The next level up list is the responder list. These are contacts that took an action from a similar type of situation. For example, a good responder list would be those that actually made a purchase from a similar restaurant in your segment.

When a contact went through the motions to take action, then the theory is that there is a high likelihood they would take the same action for your restaurant. As you can imagine, the responder list is higher priced. Higher price entails higher response rate for your mail outs.

There is an even higher level. This is the hotline list. These are recent responders. The thinking is that if the contact took a similar action in a recent period, then he or she will have a higher likelihood of repeating the same action in the recent timeframe.

A good hotline list with recent buyers of thirty days entails a higher cost. A lot of mailers balk at this level of pricing. But if you analyze the response rate and analytics, you may be surprised to find the cost per acquisition is lower with the hotline recent buyer list.

The big takeaway is to always be testing. There are stories of a mailer renting a hotline list and the return is positive. Then they do a rollout with more names and find that the numbers are dismal. This could have been the result of deceitful practices in behalf of the list company. Or this could have been a variable such as the day the letters were mailed. You just need to be constantly testing and stay on top of the numbers.

Another last tip is that the names are as implied. These names are called rentals because they are truly rented. You don't own the names until the contacts respond to your mailing and become your customers. List companies are known to seed the list with their own test contact information to make sure you are not re-mailing after the initial send-out. The contract, unless stated otherwise, is for one mailing.

Sign Twirling and Flags

This marketing nugget is sign twirling and banners. The caveat is that this concept is viable depending on city ordinance. Mine allows sign twirlers and banners on the weekend only. I have found this nugget to be effective.

A quick description of sign twirling is that a human stands on the side of a busy street holding your sign. Hence the name, the sign is being moved at all moments garnering the attention of passing cars and pedestrians. The banner flag is the same concept except it is planted into the ground. The movement of the flag catches people's eyes, and the message is read.

With sign twirling, you want to create a message that is readable but also calls for action. For example, free drink with a purchase has worked for me. Another message is "buy one get one free." Or free appetizer with purchase. Tracking is easy on this marketing nugget. At the end of the day, compare guests that acted on the sign and deduct your payment to the sign twirler. To really dial in the effectiveness, you need to consider COGS and overhead.

Sign Twirling and Flags

Testing different messages can get expensive. A cheaper way with this marketing nugget is to purchase different colored duct tape and a plastic sheet. Both are found at the big box hardware store. Create the letters with the duct tape on the plastic sheet. Instant sign.

The banners or flags are tough to track the effectiveness. Mostly because it can be pricey to create custom flags through fabricators. Instead, I just purchase preprinted, premade flags that describe the style of food being sold. Although not trackable, adding to your marketing arsenal along with the sign twirler makes for an effective package.

Vehicle Wraps

Marketing nuggets are short chunks of marketing for your restaurant. Not meant to be time consuming but just takes a small chunk of your marketing agenda. Not really considered a campaign. Although one can make a case that it fits in the overall campaign that involves the three focuses.

Vehicle wraps are a marketing nugget. These are vinyl-printed decals that wrap your vehicle. The wrap can be a certain percentage up to full coverage. Think of vehicle wraps as billboards on wheels.

Mistakes can be made with vehicle wraps. Some of these mistakes include having cutesy text or graphics that don't lend themselves to act. Acting involves responding by calling, going to a website, filling out a form, etc. Cutesy text font is hard to read and very easily can be considered branding. You are not utilizing your precious time and ad space for ego boosts or rewards. Placing the restaurant name on the vehicle is expected, but to make it your priority is going against our mantra of success.

What should be included on the vehicle wrap? One would be to have a phone number and a statement saying call now to hear our twenty-four-hour recorded message and receive a free meal. Simply call this toll-free number. Having the statement recorded message gives the prospect the heads up that it's a recording verses a live person. People are hesitant to call a new phone number and then talk to a real human that then pushes a hard sell.

Secondary, but not as important, is your WMYU statement. Probably wouldn't hurt to have some pictures or description of the food style. You need to imagine if you were driving and see your vehicle on a roadway going at various speeds. Is it readable? Does it make sense for the brief time someone sees it?

The other side benefit to vehicle wraps is that once you get to the restaurant, you can park your car next to the main thoroughfare, and it instantly becomes a billboard. You can get a lot of mileage (pun intended) from this marketing nugget.

Photo Booth

Can you dedicate a part of the restaurant for social media opportunities? If so, then a photo booth might be the answer to increasing postings on social media. All you need to do is buy or create props that are related to your niche or theme.

A couple of chairs in the corner of the room with a backdrop makes for a simple setting. Nearby are hats, glasses, pointers, and signs in which clients wear. Then they take selfies or pics of each other. And lo and behold, it gets posted on social media.

Later, you can have a contest in which clients post their favorite pics. Then there can be peer voting in which the picture with the most likes win a free meal or tickets to the movies. And the winning picture can be posted on your wall of fame.

Make sure that whatever the guests are taking picture of that the name of your business is somehow displayed. This could be in the form of the backdrop. Maybe the props can have your name on it.

Another form of the photobooth theme is to have a cutout in which guests pop their head in and other body parts through a painted front façade. For example, if you are a restaurant by the beach, you can have a cutout of people in swimsuits holding surfboards, floaters, life preservers. The head cutouts will be where the guests pop through from the back.

Think photo opportunities. You can even have oversized props in which people take pictures in front. There are doughnut establishments that have six-foot doughnuts in front of the store. There are seafood restaurants with a statue of a sailor staring out into the crowd. There is another restaurant that has an oversized chair in which people climb atop and take pictures. And everything aforementioned have signs somewhere on the prop.

Playing Spy

Secret shopper, purchase something small with cash, order delivery, send friend to purchase.

This is one of those steps you need to do as an owner for peace of mind. There will be occasions where you are not at your restaurant. When you are out, there is this conflict running through your mind about trust. Are the team members cheating? Are they pocketing tips? Are they voiding unauthorized sales? Is the quality and service reduced? Are they over-pouring or taking food?

Even if you have family members "running" the show, you can never be too comfortable. Money changes people, and when it involves real cash, hands and mind get a little weird. I had a friend owner that let her brother take care of the business every afternoon while she ran errands and gathered supplies.

Over time, he ran orders without inputting in the register. Somehow, the kitchen followed verbal meal orders and didn't suspect anything out of the ordinary. My friend suspected her brother was cheating the business and did catch him. Unfortunately, things have not been the same in the family. As of this writing, the fracture is at ten years.

Playing Spy

There are different ways to test your organization from quality to service. And in the end, you will sleep better knowing that your restaurant and the team members are running an honest ship. One of the easier ways to start is to tell your clients in a newsletter, email, or survey that you care about quality and service. If there anything that is not up to par, have them contact you immediately. Then give your personal contact information. You may even set up a special email knowing that if there is anyone contacting you to this email, it is in regard to an issue for this topic.

Another test that I like to implement is to have my friends come into the restaurant and make purchases. They are told to make a fuss over something and then report on the experience. For example, they order something and then change their mind. They receive their dish, taste it, and then send it back. The goal is to see what happens with resolving the situation. Also, my friend scores the team member on friendliness and politeness.

A test involving tips is that my friend will also tip. The serial numbers of the tip are recorded. Then, when the owner gets back, the tips are scanned for the bills with the serial number. If the bills are missing, then there might be an issue. There is a possibility that the bills were used for money exchange. You can track these episodes or clear the matter quickly.

On occasions, I also send one of my friends to purchase a small item with cash. This small item usually involves front of the house. If the kitchen gets involved, it is harder to get away with pocketing cash. This item is usually a drink. One of my other restaurant friends fired a waitress because one of his friends purchased a drink with cash. Then a short time later, my friend came into his restaurant and looked in the register for the purchase. It wasn't there.

I like to test delivery. This accomplishes two things. I use a third-party service and order a selection of items. Then the clock starts running. I test for the time it takes from order to arrival. When the food arrives, I look over the packing of the food. I usually order drinks, soups, hot food, and a salad. I check for leakage. I check for temperature.

Press Releases PR
Food challenge, wall of fame, name a food, food day,

Restaurant owner, an advocate of "Turn off your technology," gives discount for diners who turn off their cell phones. This was actually a headline in the local newspaper. But wait, there's more. The local news station picked this story up and broadcast this story on their evening and late news slots. This restaurant owner was the President of the "Turn off your Technology" advocacy group. This was a real group that comprised of himself and his team members of the restaurant.

The reason this story got noticed is because people were and still are glued to their cell phones. In my restaurant, there are diners who just look at their cell phones at every moment of the dining experience. Even on Valentine's Day, there were couples looking at their cell phones.

The above story was interesting, timely, and a little over the top. These variables helped get this restaurant exposure and publicity. Could you imagine how much it would have cost to purchase advertising slots for the times the restaurant owner's story was featured?

Publicity does not have to be a random occurrence or long odd goals. If you are mindful of everything that happens in and around your restaurant with the aspect of possibly being newsworthy, you can actually get recognized through the media channels.

There is a certain tool used and received by news reporters. This is called a press release. This press release basically tells your story. It is definitely not promotional. One can make an argument that the cell-phone-eliminating owner was offering discounts, which was promotional. However, the story was more focused on a person who was fed up with people not socializing and created an advocacy group. It just so happens that he gave rewards in the form of discounts.

In the old days, there were special publications that listed reporters and editors. These days, you can find the information online. Keep a list handy of possible contacts and start creating a newsworthy topic. It is very challenging in the beginning, for sure. You can send in a lot of press releases before you get the feel for something that might be recognized.

But your press releases don't need to be wasted. If not picked up by the news media, you can then repurpose the information for your newsletters, blogs, and social media accounts.

I was blessed with getting my restaurant featured on the Los Angeles news station. Admittedly, it wasn't planned by me. One of the waitresses found a wallet months ago and it had a sizable amount of money inside. She didn't keep the money. Instead, she put it in the drawer. Months later, a family came in and, out of the blue, inquired about possibly finding the wallet. It turns out that the wallet belonged to their five-year-old son.

Press Releases PR

The waitress returned the wallet. The grateful parents called all the news agencies and told them about the good-hearted waitress. When I walked in the restaurant that evening, there was a camera crew inside. I thought the restaurant had been robbed or someone was hurt. But the camera crew and the reporter were there to interview the waitress. Later on, on television, the story aired along with the front of my restaurant and a verbal mention.

Yes, that was luck. But you can sway the odds in your favor. Think of newsworthy stories that can relate to your restaurant and send press releases. Some ideas include an eating competition (think about how that worked with Nathan hot dogs). Maybe have a food festival. Create a special food day. Heck, there's already an ice cream day and pie day.

Remnant Space and Advertising

Making the leap to printed media can be an effective way to increase market reach. When you send for the ad-rate media packet, you soon realize that it's pricey. The ad rates are justified because readership numbers are the variable that determines this price.

Print advertising is scary because once it's printed, it's locked in. You cannot change anything until the next publication. But the upside is that it is printed and locked in. If the returns on the ad exceed cost, then it's a winner.

And even though it was for a monthly ad (varies by media and publication), there is also the opportunity for the advertisement to continue pulling months longer. Imagine a magazine on the rack for sale. People browse through magazines in retail stores. They may buy. They may not.

Then there are the magazines that are passed along. Someone reads a magazine. After reading, the magazine is passed on to a new owner. Or in the waiting room and the library, your ad can have a far reach past the original reader.

Remnant Space and Advertising

There are ways to help ease the pain of paying the listed price. You can ask for remnant space pricing. This means that any ads that aren't sold near deadlines, pricing is reduced to entice advertisers to fill that space. Sales reps will tell you that this pricing does not exist. But if you are willing to be patient, you can state that it's okay if they don't have any remnant pricing and to place you on the contact waiting list. Imply that you are very interested in advertising, but you are the company that wants a return on the dollar versus branding. You will probably get a quizzical look. Sales reps are taught to sell the ad on branding. They want to make sure that you keep advertising to build your brand and don't want anyone to realize that the ad is not returning the investment (ROI).

Lastly, tell them if, in the future, there are any unsold spaces, to give you a call. It may take several printings, but I virtually guarantee that the sales rep will call you. Even when the moment comes, you can say that you don't have the budget now and if they can help you out with the pricing. The deadline is tomorrow. I think they can work with you.

Another tactic is that if you want to get a better rate, then you can run a block of ads. The sales rep will eagerly sign you up for the multiple runs because it looks good on their end. But you do want to have a conversation about cancel policy. Most companies I worked with will say that if the ad isn't working sometime during the run, that you can cancel without penalty.

Shopping Site

T-shirts, food kits, plastic food, private label, Groupon type promotion, hats

We are living in a great time with technology. In the past, to create a shopping site with the necessary security certificates and shopping cart processes was literally a headache. Also, the cost was expensive. A programmer was often needed to set up the website. A shopping site was basically a non-consideration for the restaurant owner.

But today, we can set up a shopping site within a couple of hours. The cost is totally affordable. And the security is in place. If you don't want to integrate your merchant account, that is okay. The sites also offer merchant account usage.

Why should you consider a shopping portal? I feel the ease of entry is the primary reason. You can then brainstorm products and offerings. There are so many ways to create another income stream with products for your restaurant.

The obvious product line that comes to mind is apparel. T-shirts and hats are good products to carry. But that doesn't have to end there. Do you have a signature dish that is unique for your restaurant? You can have custom plastic food made and then offered on your shopping site. It seems that spilled glasses or glasses with fake liquid, such as beer and soda, sell for the gag aspect. And if the glass has your logo and name of restaurant, then all the better.

Remember the chapter about cooking classes? You can also sell your food kits on the site. You can also offer a subscription service to re-supply your clients with product on regular intervals.

Authority marketing can overlap with your shopping site. You can offer private-label items. Private-label products are through contracting with existing manufacturers that produce products that your restaurant and clients may use. Instead of placing their label on the product, they can place on your custom label. This gives the impression that you produced it. It adds to the perception that you are an authority in this niche. While you are at it, sell your cookbook (mentioned in another chapter) to further strengthen your authority marketing.

You can also offer gift certificates or dining vouchers through your shopping portal. You can create special limited-edition cards that will entice the buyer to purchase as a gift. Package in a tin. And offer gift wrapping as an upsell.

Table Tents

Table tents are worth mentioning. If you have been in the food and service business for a while, then you know what they are. But just to make sure, I wanted to devote a chapter on table tents just in case.

Table tents are basically small signage that you place on the table. It is called table tents because the original signs were little pieces of cardboard that were folded into a triangle and looked like a tent. Nowadays, table tents come in different shapes and materials.

Table tents work. People read them. If they are not looking into their phones, their eyes are looking and reading. I have used table tents to promote upcoming special occasions such as Mother's Day and Valentine's Day. I have used table tents to introduce new menu items such as desserts and appetizers.

I like working with vendors with table tents. This works especially well with drink vendors. They all seem to have a co-op budget in which they will provide the table tent and even the custom printing. Their printing is high end, color, and glossy. You can't duplicate that on your home printer.

Table Tents

There are some vendors that if you place their condiments exclusively on your tables, they will print and provide the carrier. Some carriers are not only multiuse with the advertising and condiment storage but also have a charging station.

Vendors know the importance of table tents. With technology, there are vendors that offer mini-tablets for the tables. Some include pay and ordering functions. But more aligned with this topic, these mini-tablets automatically scroll, via slide show, menu items. An extension is that the technology enrolls clients in rewards programs and asks them to complete surveys.

There is a caveat with table tents. They are really a chore to keep clean. Team members don't really care to clean the nooks and cranny of an intricately designed table tent. Also, crumbs tend to find a home in the most unlikely places in a table tent. Fingerprints. I cannot stop talking about the fingerprints. Clients eat finger foods and their fingers are greasy. And that is the moment that they decide to pick up a table tent to read.

Tell a Passionate Story

Telling a passionate story is a powerful component of your marketing campaigns. In fact, telling any story helps to make your establishment more human. Clients will identify with your purpose and pathway to the present and future. They want to contribute to your story by frequenting your restaurant and supporting through eating.

A passionate story describes a downtime in your life. It obviously should relate to the marketing message. Remember that you are running on ethics. You don't want to make a story up for the sake to make your clients sympathetic. There is a story within you that got you here. There was probably a downtime in your life that made you realize and turn to a different path.

One master marketer talked about his passionate story on how he was a ten-year-old supporting his family with multiple jobs. His dad passed away when he was five. His mom was a cleaning lady that didn't get home until midnight.

And yet, he overcame adversity and became a millionaire when he turned thirty. This is your rags to riches story that you probably have heard similarly from other people we consider successful. We root for the underdog.

The stories are timeless. We are humans. We can identify and relate. That is your goal. Find your passionate story. Tell and retell. Use it in your marketing. Don't be shy. Its real, and you are intimately sharing something about your life that others will respect.

But there are many uses for your passionate story. You may use it for your "about us" page on your website. You can use it in your direct mailings. In social media, your story should be in the information or bio block.

You are going to be an author? Read the chapter on authority marketing. Your passionate story extended will find its way in a larger chapter for sure. Interviews, video, blogs, and professional gatherings are all opportunities for your story. What is your story? I want to know.

The Iron Clad Guarantee

It is usually implied that when a client does not receive great service or food, then he or she is entitled to a remedy that may include re-cooking the food, discounting, or refunding. I feel that in the food service industry, this is a blanket expectation that is usually accommodated.

However, on the new client end, there is the hesitation regarding trying out a new dining experience. Humans want to stay in their comfort zone, and it takes several visits before a dining spot becomes habit. At that point, a restaurant can make a minor mistake and the client will probably understand and keep coming back.

But with the new client, there needs to be prodding or a little push to get them to act. This is usually in the form of a promotion, coupon, or gift card. But again, it's not a clear-cut response, or we would be looking at a 100 percent response rate. In that case, you can bottle up your marketing and sell the package for more than what your restaurant is making.

Therefore, at all points of the process, you need to consider how to reduce the small bumps and barriers for the client to come to your restaurant. One of these variables is to fully state your guarantee. You want to assure the client that you stand behind your product and will do whatever it takes to make the dining experience a happy memory.

There are different levels of guarantees. It is up to you to decide which level is appropriate. Each guarantee correlates to how confident you are with your service and food.

The first level guarantee is that you will fix the situation. This could be service and/or quality of food. You will try your best to correct the episode. If you can't to the client's satisfaction, you will cheerfully refund the full price paid.

The second level of guarantee incorporates the first level guarantee. But with this level, you are adding in something for their pain and suffering. Besides getting a full refund, they would receive a free dish at that time or future date. This can be done with a gift certificate or gift card.

The third level of guarantee incorporates the first level guarantee. But with third level, you will actually offer to pay the client's next meal at your competitor's restaurant. I realize this takes bravery on your part, but if you think it through, this can be an effective guarantee. If the client understands that you will actually pay for their meal at the competitor's, then they realize that you stand behind your food and service. The pain point of trying your restaurant is reduced dramatically.

Once you decide on a guarantee, you want to state it in all your marketing campaigns. This guarantee can be written into your business cards, direct mailings, signage, digital screens, and menus. The takeaway is that the more outrageous you are with your message, the more likely the client will take notice and give you their trust.

Video Channel

A video channel or a library of videos should be on your short list of marketing must dos. There are sites that host your videos for free. All you need to do is upload your videos to these sites and they are accessible from all over the world twenty-four-seven.

There are several reasons you want to create videos. The primary reason is that there are some people who like to watch videos verses any other media. They are satisfied with content that is video-related versus print and audio.

If you are in the video for most of the topic, you can be strengthening your perception of being an authority in the niche. In some instances, without trying, you can become a sort of celebrity in your area.

Videos don't need to be professionally shot. In other words, you do not need an expensive camera. Many people reading this book have a mobile phone with video capabilities. If that is the case, you can shoot short videos and immediately upload.

The good news for the food service industry is that you have many topics in which to choose from. You can spotlight team members. Each "episode" you can conduct and interview that can include interests/hobbies and specialties. You want to humanize your business where there is that connection between the team member and the viewing audience. You can have your team members dance, sing, and lip-sync.

You can create a video on how to prep your favorite dishes. Through social media, you can ask clients for their favorite dish. Or you can ask what dish they would like to see prepped and cooked on the show.

Topics on mini tours are also popular. People are fascinated with the happenings behind the scene. You can video the tour in the POV (point of view) aspect in which the viewer feels they are there versus being a bystander from afar. People like the goings on in the kitchen so much that there is actually a popular Italian chain of restaurants that offer a table in the kitchen if the guest chooses. The restaurant also gives tours to first timers that include walking into the kitchen.

Videos are also noticed by the search engines and can sometime get high rankings. When you upload the video, there will be fields in which to input the title and description. But more importantly, you are given the opportunity to enter keywords. These keywords are the words that people search for in the search engines.

Among the information for the fields, you also need to include address, city, state, and phone number because all these words are able to be indexed in the search engine. For example, if someone searches for type of food and city, the keywords will show up as bold in the rankings.

Video Channels

Another benefit of being listed in the search engines is that there is a thumbnail of the video listed. Therefore, you want the first few seconds of the video to have an interesting image or some sort of title to catch the eye. This static pic will be shown in the listing.

Window Display

This is a good opportunity for those that are in shopping centers, malls, strip malls, and similar. If there is an unleased space on the property, one can negotiate with the property manager to use the window space to create a display. This display is themed to advertise your restaurant.

This benefits both parties because the empty window is actually being occupied by something interesting. This helps you because you are capturing the eyeballs of foot traffic. If you offer a promotion that can only be found in the window, you will be able to track its effectiveness.

The ideal window display entails something with movement. It doesn't need to be complicated with animatronics, pyro effects, or multimedia wowie zowie. Rather, simple movement such as moving signs, arrows, and shapes can capture the glances of passersby.

If electricity is an issue, then another way to create an effective window display is using plastic food. Plastic food for some reason still captures attention. Having a table setup in the window with the food and drinks captures the imagination and makes impulse decision-making when there is a question on where to eat.

The window also needs to have some sort of a way to track. Having a sign or QR code with a promotion will help you know where and how the client found out about the promotion.

One of the popular promotions is to offer a free gift card. The client sees the sign in the window and follows the QR code to a special page on your website. The client then completes the form and receives the gift card in the mail. You can then track the gift card from the display window to redemption. Please see the chapter on gift cards for more details.

If you don't have access to a window location, you can still use your window for a display. The big takeaway is that the window is like a billboard. If approached with this perception, then suddenly, a spot to view the outside/inside becomes a marketing tool.

Everything mentioned previously with off-site window displays can be incorporated in your restaurant's window. But there is one more element you can add. Neon signs used to be the norm with style of signage, but it now seems like LEDs have become popular. Neon signs still have that magic glow and are bright in colors. Consider using a simple neon sign displaying a message such as type of food or service, such as delivery.

Flat screens are also a good addition to your window. There is a separate chapter on digital signs found in the book for more details.

Wooden Nickels

Wooden nickels are fun. When I was a child, I recalled businesses giving away wooden nickels. Wooden nickels are wooden discs that are larger than nickels. They are custom printed. The natural printing is the name of the restaurant and wording about redemption.

Finding vendors are not a challenge. In fact, to compete, vendors offer different options such as double-sided printing, different colors, and a serial number. In fact, you can order different shapes.

Another popular print is to place a denomination such as $1 or $2 that the client can use on their next visit. There is a tactile feeling with a wooden nickel, and it has that certain weight appeal. It looks like it was crafted versus mass produced. It just lends itself as unusual and cool.

Wooden nickels have a history. They were once used as commemoratives for fairs, events, and arcades. In the Depression (1930s), there was a shortage of actual coins. Wooden nickels were accepted as real denomination for purchase and selling.

Wooden Nickels

There is a popular wooden nickel call a "Round Tuit." The wording thread goes like, "I'll do it once I get a Round Tuit." Maybe on your wooden nickel you can have the wording, "I'm coming to your restaurant because I got a Round Tuit."

I think it's the nostalgia aspect, but using wooden nickels to bring clients back into your restaurant has great opportunities. You can give the wooden nickel to birthday recipients and new guests to entice them back. You can even give to guests that complain to resolve the situation. You can give to children in a group. They will remember the moment and definitely will ask to use it the next time the family goes out to dine.

You can use wooden nickels as an unusual business card. When people ask what you do for a living, you can hand them a wooden nickel. People will not throw wooden nickels away. It is like throwing money away. It is taboo.

You can also try to serial number the nickel and try the collecting aspect of the promotion. You can sell lucky numbers at a premium through your shopping portal or auction on a selling site.

Wooden nickels can also be used for swag bags for Chamber of Commerce events. You can use them for bumpy mailings. It is hard to throw away a mailing when it is bumpy. It is human nature to open an envelope that has an unusual bump. If you haven't offered a happy hour or mid afternoon is slow, your wooden nickel can have hours posted along with a denomination. Or you can actually call out the promotion, such as free appetizer on next visit.

Borrow and Execute

It takes time to develop ideas and campaigns. And it takes even more time to hone the skills to utilize marketing at a proficient level. The good news is that effective marketing has not changed. Humans are still humans with the same wants, desires, and trigger points.

Therefore, one of the easiest ways to create marketing campaigns is to borrow from existing advertisements. You want to dedicate a filing cabinet or digital storage for direct mail pieces, magazine ads, flyers, etc.

You need to cast a wide net because the bad news is that it will be a challenge to find such campaigns from your area and competitors. But this is also good news because they are not advertising and marketing and utilizing the powerful tools that you are learning from this book.

You don't want to collect all the ads you come across. Instead, look for the ads and marketing that have some of the elements discussed. This includes a powerful headline. Does the ad have a deadline? Does it have a call to action or some sort of offer? Are there benefits? If it feels like the advertisement is branding, then you don't want to add it to your collection.

Another important step is not to copy word for word. It is okay to get ideas and tone from the copy. But it is important that you use your own words and make it your own. For example, you can take the original headline and change the wording. You will find through testing that the headline is still effective. And you will sleep better at night knowing you didn't plagiarize someone else's work.

Did you ever notice that pizza restaurants all have the same type of ads? It's true. And so do law firms, tire companies, car dealers, and the list goes on. If you think about it for a second, when someone starts a business and then wants to get into advertising, he looks at the competition for ads. People think that if a successful business advertises and appears to be successful, it will be safe to copy the format, layout, and style.

This could be true. But on the client side of things, the ads get watered down. The client sees the same types of ads and billboards. They become numb to the same types of ads, and that can carry through to the whole segment.

One of the most powerful ways to build your files is to look to other industries. Besides observing marketing campaigns in your segments, look outside of your niche. If you are able to determine the advertisements are working for another sector, borrow and execute in yours. Oftentimes, the marketing will be fresh and clients will notice because it is different from the typical advertisements in your market.

Borrow and Execute

The question is how to determine if the campaign is successful in a different sector. Probably the easiest way is to get on mailing lists, subscribe to their contact list, and get back issues of publications. A safe bet is if the ad is continuously being run over an extended period of time, it is probably working for the company.

Copywriting 101

Did you know that a master copywriter can make millions just crafting a letter? Just imagine taking words to paper and, in return, receiving green paper with numbers. Crazy world. But I know that we are not copywriters; we are restaurant owners. And we probably don't have the money to hire a great copywriter. We must do as we do with many tasks, roll up our sleeves and complete it ourselves.

The bad news is that being a great copywriter takes dedication, experience, and perseverance. But the good news is that you can hack your way to decent copy whether it's a letter, advertisement, or similar.

Elements that should always be included in your writings start with a headline. A headline grabs the attention of the reader. Think newsy. Don't think branding. The headline should be at the top and in larger font. Headlines are not frivolous. Throughout advertising history, just changing the headline but keeping everything else the same, a campaign has gone from a losing endeavor to making millions (see www.SenseiOfSucess.com for examples of headlines).

There are many examples of proven headlines. You just need to twist and turn the wordings to fit your situation. And if you are stuck crafting a headline, it doesn't hurt to use the words "how, now, and free" in the wording.

The text should be written in a casual, conversational style. Sometimes it is helpful to record yourself talking to an imaginary client with the message you want to deliver. This message could be about your restaurant, a promotion, or an event. But make sure that a good chunk of what you are delivering benefits the client. They want to know why they should care. In other words, "What's in it for me?"

There are other elements that are required in every letter and advertisement. Make sure that every letter has a PS and signature block at the bottom. If you believe the surveys, a recipient of a letter reads the headline first. Then he or she goes immediately to the end of the letter to see who it is from. While there, the reader can't help but look at the PS. A lot of times, the PS is just the headline reworded or contains some sort of urgency, such as a deadline.

Within the letter, there should be subheadings or mini titles in bold. This helps with a reader who scans the letter rather than reading word for word. These mini titles should capture the gist of the wording in the paragraphs. For example, a mini title that reads "But Wait, There's More" describes the opportunity to receive more than the primary benefit. Another popular mini title is "Here's How to Order."

Also within the letter should be bullet points. These bullet points contain the benefits and features of what you are offering.

Many times, this area of the letter is also in bold. The wording can be fragmented. It is important that the benefits are included. You can write that this product has a feature such as "anti-lock brakes." But the benefit needs to be included, such as "protects you and your family by adding controllability in a dangerous situation, such as icy conditions."

Within the letter, if room permits, add testimonials. Testimonials add credibility. We all approach advertisements with skepticism. Testimonials help break down the barriers. The more testimonials, the better. There are some great packages that include a whole page of testimonials.

Other elements that can be included to help with reader engagement are handwritten doodles, arrows, and notes. These entail taking a pen to your typed letter and writing small notes, such as "you must see this" circled with arrows. This leads the reader to the areas of the letter that you want them to see. This could be the offer itself, the deadline, and important details.

To become even more proficient with copywriting, start compiling examples of sales materials. Now you have a purpose with your junk mail. If you start to notice repetition in mail, pull these packages aside and start collecting and referring. Industry pros call this collection "swipe files." There is another chapter devoted to this topic.

Section Three – Success Bonus Strategies / Tactics and Authority Marketing

For most of these tidbits of information, they don't really fit into any of the other sections, but they're just as important to your success, and the success of your business, as the aforementioned marketing campaigns and tactics. I'll share with you some of the secrets I've learned over the years that have kept me in a successful mindset, kept me positive, and kept me humble in my life.

It occurred to me, as I wrote this book, that the primary purpose was to impart the most important aspect of restaurant success. As you already have found out, marketing is the most important focus. However, as the words, tactics, and strategies found their way onto the pages, I realized that my own life was more than the marketing.

Please understand that marketing is still the message. However, with every marketing campaign, there are things happening in the background to ensure the effectiveness and success. It's like the engine is the reason a car moves. And gas is the reason why the engine can do what it can do.

With that said, there are chapters within this book that have nothing to do with marketing. But in a sense, they do because without recognizing and applying the information presented, the marketing will be less effective.

These chapters were written because they worked for me and continue to work effectively in my business practices, marketing, and success.

Authority Marketing

Authority marketing is the third section. This type of marketing can take time to establish and is not for the faint at heart. But to those brave souls that utilize this powerful weapon, you will reap the benefits multiplied by your efforts.

Authority marketing, as it suggests, is placing you, which is the extension of your restaurant, as the authority in the business. Personally, it doesn't take much to reach deep and look at your buying and dining habits. Have you made purchases or walked through the doors of a business because of the founder or owner? Think famous chefs, amusement parks, designers, and athletes. And when we do business with these companies, the competition and price doesn't matter. Really? $120 for one ticket to enter an amusement park? Or up to $200 for a pair of shoes?

You can do this and place your business in these categories also. Authority marketing is so detailed and deep that it would take its own book to cover the subject. However, I will describe some authority marketing as it applies to the restaurant industry. In the following, you will find adequate results to increase your bottom line.

Cooking Classes

There are several reasons why cooking classes are an awesome tool for your business. The primary reason is that it casts you in the authority spot. The clients meet the actual person behind the curtain. They are awed and oohed by your skills and the information you impart. Unless you are a twenty-four-hour operation, cooking classes can be held at your restaurant before or after closing. These may be weird hours, but you will find avid guests that love to cook. They will come to your classes.

Classes are usually offered at a very nominal price. The goal is to break even. This makes the classes more attractive to more guests (because of the hours), and you can have more participants verses a room of two.

There are different approaches to cooking classes. You can be the person that demos the cooking to an audience or actually have the audience participating with the cooking. The hands-on approach is more effective because there are those who are kinesthetic and like to create their own dishes. At the end, everyone sits down and dines together. A cool bonding experience.

You can make this aspect of your marketing fun. If there is a farmer's market nearby (getting more popular) or a market, you can have a walk through and have the participants buy their own food before going to your restaurant for the prep and cook. It is important that the event is held at your restaurant because people will be taking pics and selfies with location finder and posting on social media. Also, there will be those that signed up for your class without even knowing about your restaurant. Taking the cooking class may add a new diner to your business.

This can also be a focus two marketing weapon because the natural way to reach out to your students is by advertising in your newsletter, PIP, chalkboard, etc. Your current clients will be delighted to know you have other dimensions besides selling food.

One more very important component of your cooking class: you need to take a video of your class preparing your best and favorite dishes. With the video, you create a video-hosting site channel on the internet. Or you can package your videos in a gift package that contains utensils, pre-portioned ingredients, your proprietary sauce, etc. and use that as an additional income stream.

Cookbook

Nothing prepares a new guest (and even regular clients) when they walk into your restaurant and see a cookbook for sale that is authored by you. In our society, we place authors as authority experts. And that's a good thing because writing a book has never been easier. Even if you are challenged with writing, taking great pictures of your dishes and filling the book with recipes is not like writing a book on quantum physics.

Worst case scenario, you can hire a ghostwriter from the various freelance sites sprinkled throughout the internet. Freelancers are great at what they do, and specialized writers can produce a book of high quality.

There are printers that specialize in book printing and can print books in low volumes. Albeit the price is higher, you really cannot look at the book as a profit center. The book is a marketing tool and weapon. It will lend you credibility and marketing power like no other. If you can sell at a profit, that will be a bonus. But plan on practically giving it away. It is your credibility business card.

You can have a book signing event with your existing client list, along with a special dinner. The event is to garner referral and social media mileage. You also want to invite the members of the local Chamber of Commerce (because you are a member—right?). Another boost to this event is if you donate all book sales to your favorite charity.

A very popular format these days is to dedicate the first part of the cookbook as a mini biography. This bio will open the door as to who you are and what brought you to the present-day business. The next section are dishes from your restaurant with professional pictures and recipes. Plan on a book that is minimum of one hundred pages. Any less and the book may not be taken too seriously. A 200-page book is recommended.

Air Miles

My friends and family think that my restaurants are cash cows because I take some great vacations. I often jokingly say to my friends that I don't care if my restaurants break even. Then they look at me in a curious manner. It turns out that most, if not all, of my airfare and travels are free and paid for by my restaurants. Let me explain.

We live in a great era in which life hacks abound. This is true for travel. One of the perks of having a restaurant is that you can take full advantage of free travel through air miles credit cards. These credit cards credit you one point to every dollar you spend on your credit card. Usually, each point is worth one cent. So it takes one hundred thousand points to equal one thousand dollars toward airfare, hotels, or any other aspect of travel, although airfare is the most popular.

For the average consumer, building up points takes a while. Spending one hundred thousand dollars to get a thousand-dollar ticket seems out of reach. But if you, as a restaurant owner, use the air miles credit card for everything under your roof, air miles build up quickly.

For example, I use my credit card with the food distributor. Every week, I use my credit card to pay for all my restaurant food and supplies. Basically, my cost of goods is 100 percent air-miles driven.

I also use my credit card for vendors such as plumbing and fridge repairs, and even utilities. Utilities include phone, gas, and electric. My default question, whenever I'm about to make a payment, is if a credit card is accepted as payment.

The obvious question is how and why a credit card company would afford to do this type of reward program. Remember that credit card companies charge processing fees and even annual fees. Just know that they are making money on both ends of the transaction.

The caveat, of course, is that you have good to excellent credit. Without this level of credit, obtaining credit cards can be a challenge. If your credit score is a challenge, you can still increase your score through various tactics and strategies. The other caveat is that the credit card needs to be paid off in full every month, or you will start to accrue interest. Any interest will override any benefits you receive in air miles.

A side note: air miles cards offer other perks to help compete with the other credit card companies. For example, lounge access is one of the perks. It is a great escape when you get to a crowded airport and settle into one of the airport lounges to relax until your flight. These lounges are quiet, have free food and drinks, and often have showers to refresh from long flights.

I tell you, if you are not utilizing this perk of having a business, you are missing out. As stated before, there are many credit cards available from every major bank. It doesn't have to be air miles reward cards. There are also reward cards on cash back, hotel stays, and bonus sign-on to help you get out of your business and travel to see the world.

You are invited to peruse the back of the book for resources or access my website to get up-to-date information on credit card travel perks. Again, resources are not included in the book because by the time you read the resources it may already be outdated, or there is a better resource for you to utilize. Good marketing has worked in the past and will always work into the future. Humans are humans. That is what this book is about.

Marketing aside, there are some aspects of owning a restaurant that I feel you should know. You see, as stated before, I own (at the time of this writing) three restaurants. I wish I had known the information that I have written for you here. But I feel that you will understand the importance of this if you know the backstory.

For five or so years, I had implemented marketing into my businesses and reaped some great rewards. Besides elevating my lifestyle with travel, dining, and investments, I took for granted the flow of money coming my way. My handling the cash flow went like this. I would pay all the expenses and overhead on a daily, weekly, and monthly basis. At the end of the month, if there was money left over, it was mine to use for myself.

Reflecting, this was crazy. I know this now and want to inform you of this dangerous way of doing business. You see, with the above method, it's really hard to track what is going on. But most importantly, this process disregards the most important component of the business—the business owner. The whole reason we got into business was to be compensated, hopefully, at a level in which it is worth all the time to have a business.

Sadly, when businesses are surveyed, many business owners are getting compensated less than if they worked as an employee with a guaranteed paycheck. But our reply is that we got into this business because of freedom. Right? Maybe. But that gets old really fast when your personal bills are coming due, including the mortgage, car payments, and medical emergencies.

This chapter is one of the most important chapters in this book (all are really important). The most important sentence to take away from what I'm getting at is "to pay yourself first." Simple, really, but I know for a fact that business owners pay themselves last. If there is any money left over from all the expenses, then somehow, the extra money finds its way to the business owner. But there are more than enough times where the extra money is being pushed into repairs, upgrades, dishes, tools, and the list never ends.

Running on this endless treadmill does several things to your psyche. First, there will be a day when you will realize that running a restaurant sucks, and why are you putting in all your time to listen to all the complaints from team members, vendors, and clients? Why are you up all night after the restaurant closes to work on paperwork, billing, and government requirements? Motivation stops.

My hope is that you don't reach that point because it wasn't long ago when we all got into this business because of the fun and positive challenges that come from owning a restaurant. Every day is different. We meet some great people. We can utilize our creativity juices to create awesome food, environments, and experiences.

That changes now. Here is a simple plan in which you pay yourself first and regain the power that you had let go during the ownership years. This plan has been around for over a hundred years, maybe more. Please know that this is a simple plan, and you are invited to explore this process in more detail. But the following information should serve you well and give you the confidence that it does indeed work.

First thing you need to do is total up gross sales. You may do this on a weekly, bi-weekly, or monthly basis. Then take out sales tax (if applicable). Sales tax is not your money. Set sales tax funds aside, and pay the appropriate sales tax by the due date.

Then, with the gross sales minus the sales tax, start off with taking 1 percent off the gross sales and pay yourself this money. For example, if the gross sales were one thousand dollars, then 1 percent of this amount is ten dollars. This goes into your pocket and never goes back into the business.

The next one percent is taken out and set aside for taxes. Again, ten dollars is taken out and placed in a non-accessible place (preferably in a different bank) and used when the time comes. Another 1 percent is taken out for an account titled profit. This is a great motivator account. When you see this account growing, it helps to remind you that your business is a success, and this money can be doled out at a checkpoint of your choosing.

The preferred dividend payment is quarterly to mirror what the big companies do.

Thus far, 3 percent is taken out of gross sales. The other 93 percent is placed in an account titled expenses. This account is where you take the money and pay bills, cost of goods, overhead, and basically everything you need to pay to keep the restaurant open.

You are probably asking why 1 percent? The 1 percent is a confidence booster. Your expense account should be feeling the pain at a very minimal level at 1 percent. If the 1 percent starts to put a strain on operations, you need to step back and analyze why that is the case. If, by one quarter, the percentage level is cake, and you have excess funds in the expense account, please feel free to increase the percentage to 2 percent. The caveat is that you are not able to move backward.

There are several benefits to this pay-yourself-first plan. The most obvious is that you get paid, or should it be stated as rewarded? It's about time; you should reap the benefits of the business rather than the other way around. The other benefit is that you have your hand on the pulse of the business. As you start budgeting funds and anticipate dates, you will start to get an overall picture of funds coming in and funds going out.

The final question is when should you stop increasing the percentages? If you can increase the percentages every quarter until you reach 10 percent, then it is time to relax a little and rejoice. The final question to ask yourself is with the owner's compensation at 10 percent, is this level adequate for your level of expectations?

Air Miles

Remember, pay yourself first.

Journal Writing, Goals

Journal writing and setting goals are powerful stuff. Please realize that the universe is mysterious, and there are many things we humans cannot answer. Besides marketing, the study of physics is my topic of choice. Physics explains the world and the universe with laws, equations, and principles. But nowhere have I found what you are going to find next.

A hack that anyone can do to become successful is to emulate those that we consider successful. The caveat is that you can copy or clone each step of a successful person, but you will not become that person. We are all here to offer to this world our unique gift. But in the end, you will definitely shortcut the path to success. You will dramatically increase your chances toward success.

What is success? Everyone has a different definition and perception of the word. My take is that success is reaching your intended goal.

With that said, you will, from here on out, become a student of those that you consider successful. Within the covers of this book are many tips and strategies to help you start your path toward making a difference in this world.

I have been a student my whole life, along with being a lifelong learner. After studying the success of others a good part of my life, I have come to find commonalities. One of the commonalities of those that we consider successful is writing in journals. Just making a habit of writing every day is a success in itself. There is something about taking a good pen to good paper (no digital unless you really have to). The tactile feeling, sound, and smoothness of the pen strokes makes writing a pleasurable experience in itself.

To really supercharge the process, you will need to incorporate some components in your writing. Please know that this has worked for me and others. You are still invited to add or subtract as you see fit. If it rings true with you, that is what is important. I believe just the habit of writing is powerful.

What you should include in your daily writing are three gratitudes you are feeling. You can start off the writing with "I have gratitude for . . ." Just having the gratitude attitude adds positivity and happiness into your life. Write three passages of why you have gratitude.

The next passage is for you to determine what three happenings will make for a great day. You can start off this section of your writing with, "What would make today a great day is . . ." Then write the three things that would make your day great.

The third passage is affirmations. You want to start with the passage "I am . . ." Then write what you are or want to be. For example, you write that "I am creative and able to derive solutions to every challenge, problem, and adversity." Notice that the writing is done in such a way that you already possess the trait. You don't want to write as if you want to. You want to write it as if you have it (even though you might not yet have this trait).

Speaking of mysterious, goal setting is one of those toolsets that if you follow and do, you will also be in wonderment at how it works. It does work. But like other skillsets and hacks, goal setting should be done in a certain way to become more powerful. I usually keep a separate journal for goal setting but definitely use it in my daily journal.

The first step to goal setting is to make a list of things you want to acquire, characteristics and traits you want to be, or what you want in life, basically whatever wish you may want.

Then you want to pick the top five that you feel would make the most impact in your life. Then you want to write the goal as descriptively and detailed as possible. You also want to write it as if you already obtained the goal. For example, if you want to someday own a sports car, you would write in detail everything about the car using as much as your senses as possible, and write as if you already own it.

An example is "I own a red 911 Carrera Porsche with tan leather interior, Tiptronic gear shift, tinted windows, 500-watt stereo system with a subwoofer." There is a science to writing your goals in this manner. By writing your goals as if you already obtained it, you are imprinting it in your mind.

There is a conflict in your mind because you are stating that you already obtained the goal. But your mind feels something is wrong. There is a conflict. Your mind knows you haven't obtained the goal. But the mind doesn't want to be in conflict and will resolve the situation to be back in balance. The only way to get back in balance is to obtain the goal.

Ideally, you want to state your goals in the following ways. When you wake up in the morning, you verbally state your goal. After you state your goal, you pause and visualize experiencing the goal. Getting back to the sports car, you will state your goal and then pause and actually feel what it is like to be sitting in your sports car. You are actually smelling the leather interior and listening to the music on the sound system. You are revving the engine and shifting the gears.

After stating your goal, you will start writing in your journal the three components mentioned above and then write your goals as the last component. In the evening, before going to sleep, you want to repeat the exercise of stating your goal. Then you want to pause again and do the visualization and experience exercise.

I invite you to do a quick research on goals and goal setting. You will find many others who have found goals as powerful and just spooky how it works. The universe is weird.

Reading and Audio Book

When queried, most people would agree that CEOs of big corporations are successful. It's easy to see why because many people that hold this position earn astronomical salaries. At least, that is what is reported in the media.

There have been studies as to how and what the habits are of CEOs and others who are considered successful. Other than goals (see chapter elsewhere in this book), being lifelong learners is the other trait and characteristic.

Lifelong learners are ones that are always asking questions, always being inquisitive, and always learning new things. They are pushing the envelope of their intellectual capabilities and knowledge base.

And the underlying habit to be a lifelong learner is by being an avid reader. There has been a number being thrown around that CEOs read on average fifty books a year. That's roughly a book a week. When one thinks about how busy CEOs are, and they are reading a book a week, people shouldn't have an excuse of not having the time to read.

Reading and Audo Book

The goal is to take advantage of any spare time to learn, read, and absorb knowledge. You want to take an inventory of what you do during the day. Hopefully, the majority of your time is marketing.

If you drive a car or take public transportation, the question is what you are doing with your time? Listening to music? If you are, then you need to stop. Music is not going to help with you achieving success. You need to be thinking all the time what is the best use of your time?

In this case, listening to audio books and instruction is the best use of time whenever you don't have time to read. The best time to listen to audiobooks is when you are driving. A great resource for learning is streaming audio books. Before, it was a challenge using CDs because if you are driving, changing the CDs became a chore.

But with the advent of new technology, streaming via cellular makes the whole process of learning much easier. Do you realize with the high tuition costs of schools, you can get an education in your car for the cost of ten cups of coffee? That's incredible. I hope you realize the power of learning and the ease of access to some of the best information in the world.

Tithing and Donating

The universe is mysterious. There are just some things and happenings that cannot be explained. Elsewhere in this book, this topic of the mysterious universe has been mentioned.

I feel that we were all here, taking up oxygen, but here to offer a unique gift. Minimally, we are here to make this a better world. We are obligated to do something that will not waste oxygen.

The common thread is that we are here to help those that are not as fortunate as we are. You are reading this book. You are living a life in high regards. I don't know your situation, but you are probably reading this book because you own a restaurant or maybe a business.

Think about others that are less fortunate. If you are not humbled by where you are now and where you are headed, I plead that you purchase a ticket to the other side of the world to see how others are living. The conditions people have subscribed to is really sad and really unforgiving.

It is our obligation to make this world a better world. With that said, this chapter is an attempt to taking a step toward that direction. But the unplanned upside is remarkable in itself. This is a mysterious world.

Here is my prescription. For every dollar that comes into your life, you set aside 10 percent. For example, in this case, you will set aside a dime. For every $100, you set aside $10. Ten percent is easy math.

Then you take that 10 percent and donate it to a cause. It could be your church, world organization, environmental and animal charity, or food bank; the list is endless. The money you donate goes a long way toward making this a better world for sure. The tip is to pick a charity that rings true to your heart.

This is where the mystery of the universe comes into play. But remember that you are not donating to take advantage of this benefit. It is just a happy byproduct. You are still giving from your heart, not for any self-gain.

You see, by you donating to a charity or organization, sometime in the future, your generosity is returned. And usually, its earned interest and multiplied. For example, you donate $10 to a charity. Sometime in the future, that $10 is returned with interest. In this example, it could be $15.

The caveat is that you cannot readily see the return on your money. It is only with periodic reflection and inventory of your life that you will find that your bank account is getting bigger, you are getting more sales, your business is growing, and your financial worth is increasing. It's incredible. Remember to have the gratitude attitude.

10 Percent Rule

This is one of the most important chapters that you will read in this book. It's simple and short. And when followed has some powerful effects on your life and your family and friends. Most people unfortunately retire on a level that would be considered poverty.

Think about this and reflect on your current situation. Think about acquaintances and their family and friends. Chances are you know of someone who has retired and is having a challenging situation. Some have even gone back to work out of necessity. It's sad that we live in this great country and world with all the opportunities, and yet, we have the poverty levels and elderly being in stressful situations because of a lack of money.

You are going to learn a simple step-by-step method that virtually guarantees financial success. And when started early, the result is that you can retire earlier. It's called the 10 percent rule.

The 10 percent rule states that whatever money comes into your life, you take ten percent off the top and pay yourself first. The other 90 percent is for paying the bills and just sustaining your lifestyle.

10 Percent Rule

The 10 percent you take from your income is used for investments. There are only two investments to consider. These are real estate and the stock market. Historically, these two financial tools have stood the test of time by appreciation growth. With real estate, you want to think about real estate appreciation and rental income. With the stock market, you are thinking value but also dividend income.

There are a couple of key points. First, this is a one-way street. Once you take the 10 percent, you invest, and you don't touch it until you reach a level in which it can sustain itself with returns, such as rental income or dividend returns. Only you can determine what that level is.

Some people can retire off of $500,000. Others can retire off $1,000,000. But you need to do an honest assessment, and this could change through time.

People that have followed the 10 percent rule have been able to retire in their fifties. Others have been able to retire at the standard mid-sixties but then not have to worry about money for the rest of their lives.

To empathize, you cannot cash out these investments until you retire. It is very easy to be sidetracked and be attracted to the shiny object. This shiny object can be a new sports car, the spur of the moment vacation, a medical emergency. You just need to be firm and strong and not be swayed.

The caveat is that it will take a long time for the money to grow. We are talking twenty to thirty years. But after these benchmark years, you will suddenly see tremendous growth in your investments.

This is because of the compounding of your money finally taking hold. If you look at a graph of your money growth, it is flat for most of the years. Then at year thirty, it spikes up. People call this a hockey stick graph because the graph looks like a hockey stick.

Ten percent is often touted because most everyone can spare 10 percent of their income. However, you can increase your contribution. Increasing your contribution to your investments cuts the years of compounding. Do some calculations and get excited. Set your contribution growth as one of your goals. You are creating and writing your own future. No guess work. It's automatic.

Conclusion – War Room

It's a tough battle. You are in a war. There are internal and external battles. There are product and service issues and challenges. There are regulations. There is paperwork. If you have delegated these battles to someone else, I admire you. But I know many small business owners who just do it for themselves. Maybe because of the cost to hire, or like many owners, there is the perception of no one can do it like the owner. But there comes a time where you need to put systems in place and let go a little bit. Start delegating some of these tasks and buy your freedom. Time is limited. It's a finite resource. Keep that in mind. But for now . . .

Marketing is a tough battle. It can really get depressing seeing a well-thought-out marketing campaign executed and then nothing. But marketing is a test of perseverance. You need to stay in the game and push through it. You need to test, test, and more test. I promise that you will start to compile an arsenal of marketing weapons that work for you.

Part of staying in the game is to make this game a game. My writing skills are awesome. Anyways, I try to make marketing a game so that it gives me that extra energy to just push through. I think it's in our DNA to pursue life as a game. And if it is pursued in this manner, life becomes more enjoyable.

Therefore, I try to make the process of marketing a game. For example, a dedicated space in one of my restaurants (I call headquarters) is my "war room." Just to let you know that I'm purely analog. I like to work with pen and paper. I have embraced technology. But the technology is in the background.

In my war room is an eight-foot-long pushpin board. The cork board is divided into three sections. And on top of each section are mini signs. The first section is titled "DO." The second section is titled "DOING." The third column section is titled "DONE."

I always have a list of marketing campaigns that I want to develop and execute. It could be on any one of the three focuses. Once I get a viable idea and concept, I write the details on an index card and pin it under the first column "DO."

Once I start the marketing process of this concept, I move the index card under the column "DOING." And once the marketing is executed, I move the index card under the column titled "DONE." The caveat is that it is not really done. Remember that you still need to analyze the campaign and check for effectiveness by return on investment.

The reason I like this process is that it is mentally satisfying to move the index card to the right, and finally, at the last column. I tend to keep the index cards pinned on the last column for at least a year so that I can do a yearly "pat on the back" review of my accomplishments. However, if at the end of the year I see many cards in the first column verses the last column, I am kind of hard on myself. There is a mental anguish to improve and do better.

This book is about marketing, but as a side note, I do use this war room board to strategize about other aspects of the restaurants. For example, I have index cards on future menu items, dining room improvements, team processes, miscellaneous tasks, etc. I do color code each category by using different colored index cards or color of ink. This is very helpful to home-in on what is planned, in process, and completed for the restaurant operations.

Acronyms

I also made up my own terms to help with this marketing game. For example, "MDM" stands for Massively Decisive Marketing. The universe is a strange place. Many phenomena are unexplained. This following process is no exception. It seems that the universe rewards speed verses slow. Think of the many million-dollar ideas you've had throughout your life. Then, once you seriously consider action on it, someone else beat you to the market. Happens to everyone. Speed trumps slow.

In history, especially war, speed trumps slow. Think of World War II. The Germans called it Blitzkrieg. The plan was to quickly sweep through Europe and take all the countries in a relatively short time. They were successful until the plan was slowed down. This happened when the Germans tried to take Russia.

There are two important points as to why I coined "MDM." Again, the universe rewards speed. When I plan a marketing campaign, I label it as an MDM. This reminds me to implement this idea quickly. The chances of success are improved. Also, I have reduced the time spent on this concept. I can then move on to the next marketing campaign. I bought myself more time. Remember, time is finite. Also, if the campaign is not as successful as anticipated, then psychologically, I am not negatively affected as if I had worked on the project for an extensive amount of time.

I have coined other acronyms, and not coincidentally, they all include the letter M. For example, I have Test Marketing Map (TMM). This acronym is an offshoot of the primary marketing campaign. Testing is important, and TMM is a test of a variable such as headline or promotion. It is also on an index card and usually resides in the second column "DOING."

Another acronym is Motivational Word Map (MWM). These are quotes, mostly motivational, that just give me the energy to proceed with positive expectations and confidence. This is usually on an index card and pinned to the border of my war room corkboard.

You can see that a game can be created with marketing and life. I invite you to use my methods or create your own that resonate with your psyche and soul. It's a tough world out there. Making a game out of it rounds off the edges of seriousness.

Final Note

There is a chapter in this book titled Copywriting 101 in which I write that a reader of a sales letter reads the headline first and then the signature block and postscript (PS). I suspect the same process holds true for a book. I do the same. I read the table of contents and then jump to the back of the book for resources and then conclusion. So I apologize to those who read my book from page one to the end without skipping around and this kind of reads like the introduction.

My hopes are that you will take to heart that marketing is the most important part of the three-legged stool of restaurant operations and success (the other two legs are product and service). Everything written in this book is based on my experience with success with restaurants because I own and apply everything I wrote.

My writing skills really do suck, and I write as if I'm talking with you face to face. But please, overlook that and consider the information verses the grammar. My sincere hope is that you start the marketing processes now. If you are already marketing at some level, there is always room to increase.

Final Note

There is a saying that the teacher is also the student. The teacher can learn as much or more from the student than the teacher teaches. I consider myself the student and welcome any suggestions, ideas, and questions you may have. You are invited to reach out to me at srcworld@gmail.com.

Restaurants are one of the most fantasized businesses to start, and once started, one of the quickest to shut down. Here's a true story. This happened twenty years ago, but it could have easily happened yesterday. One of my best friends had two brothers. Their dad passed away and left a small fortune. The three brothers thought it would be awesome to start a restaurant as a dedication to their father. They chose a building and spent all the money building it out. Once completed, the restaurant was immaculate. However, it was over budget and six months late opening. This was due mostly because of city regulations, inexperience, permits, and the other details that really no one considers until it happens.

Once the restaurant opened, the business shuttered in eight months. The three brothers didn't have the working capital to keep the restaurant running. There is an axiom that you need at least one year's worth of working capital to keep a new restaurant open. In other words, it takes one year before a new restaurant gains traction and is able to sustain itself.

Today, the three brothers don't talk to each other because of all the fighting that happened while the restaurant was open. After the restaurant closed, a big chain company swooped in and opened their restaurant with a fraction of what they spent that would have otherwise occurred from a ground up build.

Final Note

Why did I write about this true story? First, this happened to one of my best friends. At the time, I didn't own any restaurants, but I was practicing marketing with other products in different industries. My regret today is that I didn't help him with marketing his restaurant. I am sure that my marketing skills at the time wouldn't have hurt and maybe would have helped to prolong their staying open.

Now that I myself own restaurants, I empathize with other mom-and-pop operations. I know that marketing is the last of our considerations when running a restaurant. Food, location, service—right? I hope that you read or have read this book and keep pursuing your education in this important aspect of restaurant success.

And even in the end, if you hand off the responsibility to another person whose title is "marketing specialist" or "marketing engineer" or any title that sounds important, you will be able to speak the speak and walk the walk. You will know some of the background skillsets that are essential to restaurant success and be able to create your own pathway to happiness.

Resources

Where do we go from here? This book was written without detailed resources. Why? Nothing frustrates me more when I follow a resource from other books and the resource is gone or outdated. This book was written with timeless information. You can use this book today, tomorrow, and into the future.

As mentioned in parts of the book, I have a website. This website is the resource that you need to go to in order to get up-to-date information. Some of the resources, I use for my restaurants. Other resources are through my colleagues and friends in the business.

This book was written with strategies and concepts that you can use to help with the success of your restaurant. Your job is to take action and implement. Constantly check back to my website at:

www.SenseiOfSuccess.com

If, somehow, this resource disappears (hopefully I won't be a hypocrite), you are invited to contact me directly at srcworld@gmail.com. I've had this email for decades, and it won't disappear anytime soon. Just do me a favor and in the title section write the word SOS book, restaurant book, or something similar.

And finally, I apologize for not including actual exhibits or examples of marketing strategies and concepts. And I apologize for not giving step by steps (especially for the internet strategies). This was a struggle. But in the end, I decided to write a book with valid marketing weapons and forgo the examples because of keeping the book at a price point that would be accessible to more restaurant owners.

Also, I'm always testing myself. My goal is to always beat my previous marketing (term "control" in marketing circles). I wanted to write this book with timeless information instead of dynamic content that is changing constantly.

However, there is information on how to access my current marketing materials and examples by going to www.SenseiOfSuccess.com.

I wish you the best of luck in your pursuit towards a successful future.

Thank you.

www.ingramcontent.com/pod-product-compliance
Lightning Source LLC
Chambersburg PA
CBHW021813170526
45157CB00007B/2567